The Blossoming of
the **Yullyeo Flower**
of Heaven

| 천상의 율려 조화꽃을 피우다 |

[한영대역]

천상의 율려 조화꽃을 피우다
The Blossoming of the Yullyeo Flower of Heaven

발행일 2025년 12월 8일 초판 1쇄
저자 안경전 | **발행처** 상생출판 | **발행인** 안경전
주소 대전시 중구 선화서로 29번길 36(선화동)
전화 070-8644-3156 | **팩스** 0303-0799-1735
출판등록 2005년 3월 11일(175호)
홈페이지 https://www.sangsaengbooks.co.kr
ISBN 979-11-91329-60-5

Korean-English Edition

The Blossoming of the Yullyeo Flower of Heaven

천상의 율려 조화꽃을 피우다

무병장수 선려화 仙呂花 치유수행

Lecture and Guided Meditation by
Ahn Gyeong-jeon

상생출판

차례

Table of Contents

들어가기

현재 지구상에서 꽃을 피우는 식물이 얼마나 되는 줄 아십니까? 세계적으로는 26만여 종으로 알려져 있으며, 우리나라에는 3천여 종으로 기록되어 있습니다.

과연 여러분은 이 수많은 꽃 중에서 어떤 꽃을 가장 좋아하십니까? 나름대로 마음속에 꽃을 하나 정하셨다면, 다음 말씀을 한번 음미해 보시겠어요?

> 상제님께서는 사람이 많이 있을수록 좋아하시니라. 임인(1902)년에 하루는 상제님께서 아랫목에 앉으시어 윗목에 모인 성도들을 바라보시며 "너희들, 심심하면 심심풀이 좀 해 봐라." 하시거늘 성도들이 꽃타령을 부르니 "너희들은 꽃 중에 무슨 꽃이 좋으냐?" 하고 물으시니라.
>
> 이에 누구는 '나락꽃이 좋다.' 하고 누구는 '목화꽃이 좋다.' 하고, 또 누구는 '담배꽃이 좋다.' 하거늘 상제님께서 말씀하시기를 "방안꽃이 제일이니라. 다른 것은 한 번 보고, 두 번 보고 하면 사랑이 멀어지는 법이나 사람은 볼수록 정이 드는 것이니 참으로 꽃 중에는 인간꽃이 제일이니라." 하시니라. (道典 8:2:1~6)

Introduction

Do you know how many flowering plants there are on earth? There are thought to be more than 260,000 plant species in the world, with more than three thousand recorded in Korea.

Which flower do you like most among them? Once you've chosen a flower in your head, try to savor the following passage:

> Sangjenim loved the company of people, the more the better.
>
> One day in 1902 (DG 32) as Sangjenim was sitting in a room with the disciples, gazing upon them, he said, "If you are bored, do something to amuse yourselves." So, the disciples sang a song about flowers, and Sangjenim asked them, "Of all the flowers, which do you like best?"
>
> "Rice flowers," someone answered. Another said, "Cotton flowers." Yet another answered, "Tobacco flowers."
>
> Sangjenim declared, "Flowers that bloom inside the home are the best. Affection for an object wanes after it is beheld once or twice, but affection for people grows each time they are beheld. Indeed, among all flowers, the human flower is the best." (Dojeon, 8:2:1-6)

현재 지구상에서 꽃을 피우는 식물이 얼마나 어떠십니까? 여러분이 어떤 꽃을 좋아하는 것과 상관없이 '참으로 꽃 중에는 인간꽃이 제일'이라는 상제님의 말씀이 가슴에 와닿지 않으신지요?

지난 2022년 11월 6일 서울을 시작으로 대전(11.12), 광주(11.20), 부산(11.26)를 거쳐 대구(12.10)를 마지막으로 〈대한 영성문화 대축제〉가 열렸습니다. 그 축제에서 상제님이 말씀하신 '빛의 인간 인간꽃'이 될 수 있고 반드시 되어야만 하는 궁극의 꽃의 문화 시대가 선포되어 개화하기 시작하였습니다. 바로 무병장수 선려화 치유 수행이 전 세계에 소개되고, 그 비법이 전수되었습니다.

이제 전 지구촌에 대한인의 원형 뿌리문화와 치유문화를 아낌없이 나눠 누구라도 빛의 인간·신선의 몸·후천 인간으로 거듭날 수 있도록 상생월드센터의 동방신선학교가 출범하였습니다.

그동안 STB 〈상생개벽뉴스〉에서 치유·생존·도통의 핵심을 품은 동방 한국의 1만년 무병장수 삼신조화 수행법의 공개로 지금은 천지의 대변혁을 앞둔 병란 개벽기라는 시대상에 눈을 떴으리라 확신합니다.

What do you think? Regardless of which flower you like personally, weren't you touched by what Sangjenim said—that "the human flower is the best?"

We first held the Daehan Spiritual Culture Festival in Seoul on November 6, 2022, then took the festival to Daejeon (November 12), Gwangju (November 20), Busan (November 26), and Daegu (December 10). At these cities, we announced the dawning of the new era of the 'Flower of Light' culture, the era in which humans can and must become the human flowers of light that Sangjenim mentioned. We did this by teaching to the world the concept of Seollyeohwa ("Flower of Immortality") healing meditation for attaining ageless longevity.

We are now launching the Eastern School of Immortality Meditation as part of the Sangsaeng World Center to globally spread the archetypal root culture and healing culture of the Korean people. By doing so, we can ensure that anyone, no matter who they are, will have the chance to be reborn as humans of light with ageless bodies—humans of the Later Heaven.

STB's Sangsaeng Gaebyeok News has been spreading awareness of Korea's ten-thousand-year practice of Samsin meditation for eternal health and longevity that encompasses the core aspects of healing, survival, and enlightenment. I have the utmost conviction that, in doing so, we are opening people's eyes to the dominant theme of our times: the *gaebyeok* era of the disaster of disease that shall precede the great overturning of heaven and earth.

따라서 병란을 대비하고 2만 5천년 전 마고성에서 발원한 신선문화를 더욱 적극적으로 배워 빛꽃 도통수행을 생활화, 체질화해야만 합니다. 이와 함께 천지부모이신 아버지 상제님과 어머니 태모님의 무극대도 조화법을 날마다 깨쳐, 후천 상생의 새 역사의 주인공 빛의 인간꽃 삼랑선이 되시길 축원합니다.

도기 153⁽²⁰²³⁾년 2월 21일
증산도 종도사 안 경 전

Therefore, we must prepare for this disaster of disease and more actively study the culture of immortality that emerged in Mago Castle twenty-five thousand years ago so that we can make enlightenment meditation for the blossoming of the flower of light a habit—make it an integral part of our daily lives. I hope that by achieving a daily awakening to Father Sangjenim and Mother Taemonim's principles of the creation-transformation of the Supreme Dao of Mugeuk, you will become human flowers of light—will become the Samrang immortals who will carve out the new history of *sangsaeng* in the Later Heaven.

February 21, 2023 (Dao Year 153)
Ahn Gyeong-jeon
The Jongdosa of Jeung San Do

13

본서의 주요 술어

수승화강水昇火降
인간 몸속에서 태수太水 기운은 위로 끌어올리고 태화太火의 기운은 아래로 내려서 서로 순환시키는 것. 우리 몸속의 해와 달, 수화가 교류되어야 몸의 생명 활동이 건강하게 지속됨.

광선光仙 **아기**
일곱 성령님의 조화 광명 기운을 받아 수행자의 하단에서 잉태되어 태어난 영적 아기. 수행자를 닮은 인격신으로서 몸과 마음을 관리하는 내부 감독자이며, 수행 과정을 함께 하는 영원한 진리의 동반자.

병란病亂
우주의 여름에서 가을로 바꾸는 하추교차기에 선천 상극의 묵은 기운을 총체적으로 정리하고 인종씨를 추려서 상생의 새 우주 질서를 열기 위한 가을개벽의 통과의례. 인간의 능력으로는 도저히 극복할 수 없는 병으로, 필수불가결한 큰 정화의 과정.

삼신조화신주三神造化神珠
상제님과 태허령님의 법신法身의 손길을 상단에 모셔서 만들어진 백광의 여의주.

Main Terms in This Text

ascending water, descending fire
In the human body, Great Water energy is drawn upward while Great Fire energy descends. The two circulate in this manner. The sun and moon, and fire and water, must interchange in the human body in this way for its vital activities to carry on in a healthy manner.

baby of light
A spiritual infant who is gestated and born in the lower *danjeon* of a meditator after they receive the Seven Holy Spirits' radiant energy of creation-transformation. This is an anthropomorphic spirit who resembles the meditator and who acts both as: an internal supervisor managing the body and mind of the meditator; a constant companion in the pursuit of truth who shares in the meditation process.

disaster of disease
An inevitable process of the Autumn Gaebyeok that occurs during the transition period from cosmic summer to cosmic autumn. During this process, the old energy of the Early Heaven's order of *sanggeuk* ("mutual conflict and domination") is swept away and the seeds of humanity are selected to begin the new cosmic order of *sangsaeng* ("mutual life-bettering and life-saving").

Divine Pearl of Samsin Creation-Transformation
The luminous white wish-fulfilling pearl created as the hands

언청계용신言聽計用神

나의 말을 들어주고 나의 계획을 성취시켜주는 망량신. 수행자의 정성에 응해 몸속 일월日月인 태수, 태화 기운이 조화롭게 일체되어 생성하는 내 몸의 망량신.

정신혼백精神魂魄

인간 몸속의 신장(1水, 정精), 심장(2火, 신神), 간장(3木, 혼魂) 폐장(4金, 백魄)에 각각 깃들어 있는 우주의 영적 요소. 시천주 주문은 우주의 정신을, 태을주 주문은 우주의 혼백을 내려준다.

개벽開闢

'천개지벽天開地闢'에서 온 말. 천지는 춘하추동 4계절로 끊임없이 새로운 시간 질서를 열면서 돌아가는데 그 변화의 마디를 일컫는 말.

임맥任脈/ 독맥督脈

동양의학에 따르면, 임맥은 신체의 음陰의 에너지를 주관하는 맥으로서, 회음혈에서 승장혈까지 몸의 전면 정중앙을 흐릅니다. 독맥은 신체의 뒷면 정중앙을 흐르는 맥으로, 신체의 양陽

of the dharma bodies of Sangjenim and the Holy Spirit of Great Emptiness meet in the upper *danjeon*.

eoncheong-gyeyongsin spirits
The *mangnyang* spirits that listen to prayers and help bring plans to fruition. These are *mangnyang* spirits living in the human body that respond to a meditator's devoted meditation and that are created through the harmonious integration of the sun and moon (Great Water and Great Fire) within the meditator's body.

essence, spirit, heavenly soul, and earthly soul
The spiritual elements of the universe that reside respectively within the kidneys (1 water, essence), heart (2 fire, spirit), liver (3 wood, heavenly soul), and lungs (4 metal, earthly soul). The Sicheonjuju Mantra endows the meditator with the essence and spirit of the universe, while the Taeeulju Mantra endows the meditator with the yang soul (aka, 'heavenly soul') and yin soul (aka, 'earthly soul') of the universe.

gaebyeok
A term derived from *cheongae jibyeok* ("the new beginning of heaven and earth"). This term describes the shifts between the cosmic seasons of spring, summer, autumn, and winter within heaven and earth's perpetual cycle of change.

Conception Vessel/ Governing Vessel
In Eastern medicine, the Conception Vessel is defined as the primary energy channel regulating the body's yin energy. It runs along the midline of the anterior body, extending from the perineum to the point just below the lower lip. The Gov-

의 에너지를 관장하며 회음에서 시작하여 백회를 지나 인중까
지 이어집니다.

하단下丹

배꼽 아래 5cm 지점에서 안(등)쪽으로 2/3 정도 들어간 지점
에 있는 무형의 공간. 우주의 기氣의 통로.

망량魍魎

'망량은 빛으로 충만하여 영원한 존재'라는 의미. 우주의 무형
의 조물주 본체신이 삼신망량.

중단中丹(명단命丹)

인간 몸속에 내재해 있는 조물주의 신神과 정精의 열매자리. 가
슴의 중앙에 위치하며 수명줄이 깃들어 있는 자리.

충맥衝脈

인간 몸의 제일 아래에 있는 회음會陰에서 머리 위 백회百會까지
를 관통해서 기운이 오르내리는 도로망.

송과선松果腺

머릿속 상단上丹에서 신도神道세계로 들어가는 입구. 좌뇌와 우
뇌 사이에 있는 쌀알 크기의 송과선에 주문을 집중해서 읽으면
면 문이 열리면서 신도세계로 들어가게 됨.

erning Vessel is defined as the primary energy channel regulating the body's yang energy. It travels along the midline of the posterior body, beginning at the perineum, ascending through Baihui, and continuing to the philtrum.

lower *danjeon*
An intangible location at a point five centimeters below the navel and about two-thirds of the way inward (toward the back). A portal for receiving cosmic energy.

mangnyang spirits
The term *mangnyang* means "eternal being filled with light." The primal spirits who were the formless creators of the universe are known as Samsin Mangnyang ("The Three Primal Spirits").

middle *danjeon* (life *danjeon*)
The culmination of Samsin's spirit and essence within the human body. It is located in the center of the chest and contains a person's 'thread of longevity.'

penetrating vessel
The vertical pathway for energy to move through the human body, extending from the perineum at the bottom of the torso to the crown chakra at the top of the head.

pineal gland
The entrance to the spirit realm located within the upper *danjeon* of the head. Chanting mantras while focusing on the rice-grain-sized pineal gland between the left brain and the right brain opens the door to the spirit realm.

삼랑三郎

삼신 상제님을 섬기고 그 가르침을 따르는 수행자로써 삼신의 빛과 생명력을 회복하여 삼신 상제님의 뜻을 실현하는 일꾼.

삼신三神

천지 만물을 낳은 무형의 조물주 하나님(원신元神, 본체삼신). 삼신은 구체적으로 '태허령太虛靈님, 태성령太聖靈님, 태광령太光靈님'으로 존칭. 행촌 이암 선생은 삼신을 조화신·교화신·치화신으로 체계화함.

삼신상제三神上帝

천상보좌에서 천계, 지계, 인계, 신계를 주재하고 통치하는 유형의 조물주 하나님(주신主神). '삼신일체상제'의 줄임말.

선려화仙呂花

마고 삼신할머니가 모든 인간을 신선으로 만들어 주려는 은총으로 내려주신 귀한 축복의 선물. 우주의 율려꽃, 빛꽃으로서 본래 이름은 선정화仙定花.

상단上丹(신단神丹, 성단性丹)

머리 안 앞 윗쪽에 위치한 우주의 신神의 세계로 들어가는 관문. 머리 자체는 작지만 '신神의 집'이며 영적으로는 우주를 담

Samrang
Meditators who worship Samsin Sangjenim. They meditate to recover the light and life force of Samsin.

Samsin
The formless creators who give birth to all things in heaven and earth (aka, the 'Three Primal Spirits,' 'Primal Samsin'). More specifically, the Three Primal Spirits or Samsin are known as the Holy Spirit of Great Emptiness, the Holy Spirit of Great Holiness, and the Holy Spirit of Great Radiance. Master Yi Am (honorific name: 'Haengchon') also systematically defined these three spirits of Samsin using the titles Spirit of Creation-Transformation, Spirit of Edification, and Spirit of Governance.

Samsin Sangje
The Supreme God who presides and rules over heaven, earth, the human world, and the spirit world from his throne in heaven. This is an abbreviation of the term "Sangje Who Is One with Samsin."

Seollyeohwa ("Flower of Immortality")
The precious gift bestowed by Grandmother Mago to make all humans immortals. This is the cosmic *yullyeo* flower and the flower of light originally known as the 'Seonjeonghwa' ("Immortality Decider Flower").

upper *danjeon* (spirit *danjeon*, nature *danjeon*)
The gateway to the cosmic spirit realm located in the forehead between the eyebrows. Though the human head itself is small, it is the 'house of the spirits' and is spiritually tanta-

는 공간에 해당함.

광선여의봉光線如意棒
삼신상제님 법신의 빛실과 태허령님의 빛실을 받아 내려 내 뜻 대로 충맥과 임독맥을 정화하고, 아픈 곳을 자가 치유할 수 있도록 만든 빛(광선)봉.

천지공사天地公事
우주의 가을철을 맞아 인간으로 오신 우주의 통치자 상제님께서 인간과 신명을 데리고 선천의 병든 삼계(천지인)를 뜯어고치고 미래의 새 문명사회를 짜 놓으신 것의 총체.

무극無極
대우주가 생겨나온 근원이자 태극의 바탕 자리. 내적으로 경계가 없고 외적으로 한계가 없는 상태를 일컫는다. 증산 상제님의 진리를 '무극대도'라고 일컫는데, 이는 우주의 이법을 바탕으로 인류를 후천 세상의 궁극의 성숙, 통합, 조화로 이끄는 무극無極의 가르침이라는 뜻이다.

도수度數
'도수'라는 용어는 하늘, 땅, 인간의 변화의 질서를 나타낸다. '도수'는 또한 상제님 또는 태모님께서 가을개벽과 후천까지의

mount to a space that contains the universe.

wish-fulfilling rod of light

A staff of light for self-healing, formed by combining rays of light from the dharma bodies of Samsin Sangjenim and the Holy Spirit of Great Emptiness. Used to purify the penetrating, governing, and conception vessels at the meditator's will.

Work of Renewing Heaven and Earth

Sangjenim, God the Ruler of the Universe, incarnated just before the cosmic autumn. This term is used as a summation of his work, conducted with the aid of humans and spirits, to renew the diseased three realms (heaven, earth, and humanity) of the Early Heaven and establish the template for the new civilization to come.

Mugeuk

Romanized from Chinese as *Wuji* or *Wu-chi*. Mugeuk refers to the primordial origin of the universe and the foundational state from which Taegeuk (*Taiji* or *T'ai-chi*) arises. Literally, Mugeuk signifies a state without internal boundaries and without external limits. Sangjenim's teaching is called the 'Supreme Dao of Mugeuk,' for it is the dao of boundlessness based on the cosmic principles that guides humanity toward ultimate maturation, unification, and harmony in the Later Heaven.

dosu

The term *dosu* represents the order of change concerning heaven, earth, and humanity. It also describes plans or milestones Sangjenim or Taemonim set in place to guide the

역사의 과정을 결정하신 계획 또는 이정표를 말한다.

조화造化

생명을 낳고, 기르고, 발전시키는 우주의 본질적인 성스러운
힘으로, 하늘과 땅, 인간과 신명, 그리고 우주의 만물을 통치하
시는 상제님께서 쓰시는 권능이다. '조화'라는 용어는 또한 현
실을 자유자재로 변화시키는 지혜와 힘, 권능을 내포한다.

마고麻姑

태고 문명 시대에 인류에게 우주의 모든 소리의 근원인 '옴Om'
을 비롯, 선려화 빛꽃 수행법을 전수해주신 분이 바로 '마고 할
머니'로 불리는 마고대성麻姑大成이다. '마고성麻姑城'은 마고대성
의 가르침과 수행법을 따르고 실천하던 고대인들이 살던 곳으
로, 현재의 러시아 사하공화국 일대라고 전해진다. 마고대성과
두 따님 궁희 마마, 소희 마마—세 분은 고대 여신문화의 근간
이 되었으며, 그들의 역사는 『부도지』와 『환단고기』 등의 사서
에 전해진다.

course of history leading to the Autumn Gaebyeok and into the Later Heaven.

Creation-Transformation
The universe's innate divine power to create, nurture, and advance life, a power wielded by Sangjenim, who reigns over heaven, earth, humans, spirits, and all other existence in the universe. The term 'creation-transformation' also connotes the wisdom, power, and authority to retransform reality at will.

Grandmother Mago
Grandmother Mago, also known as Empress Mago of Grand Fulfillment, transmitted to humanity the sacred sound "Om"—the origin of all cosmic resonance—during the age of archetypal civilization. She also bestowed the Seollyeohwa ("Flower of Cosmic Light") meditation practices, guiding ancient people toward a life of spirituality and longevity. The people who followed her teachings dwelled in Mago Castle, believed to have been located in what is now the Sakha Republic of Russia. Grandmother Mago and her two daughters, Gunghee and Sohee, were the basis of ancient goddess culture, and their legacy is recorded in texts such as *Budoji* and *Hwandangogi*.

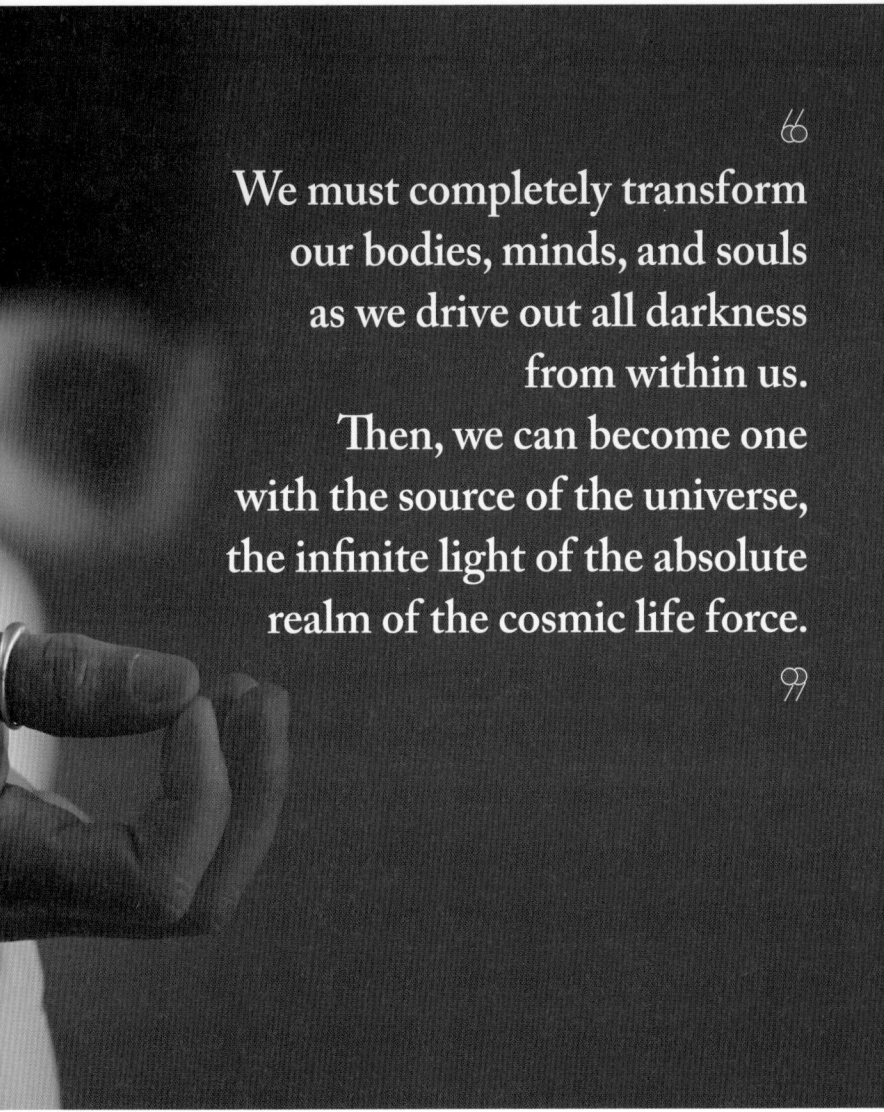

66

We must completely transform
our bodies, minds, and souls
as we drive out all darkness
from within us.
Then, we can become one
with the source of the universe,
the infinite light of the absolute
realm of the cosmic life force.

99

인간 생존의 바탕, 수행과 도통

Meditation and Enlightenment

인류 원형 도통 수행법의 핵심

오늘 이곳 대구에 모이신 분들의 기운이 밝고 좋습니다. 만나서 반갑습니다.

우리 인간의 삶과 생명에서 가장 소중한 곳이 하단田丹입니다. 하단의 정精은 우리 몸의 생명의 동력이기 때문입니다. 이 신비로운 기운이 내 몸에서 고갈되면 모든 것이 끝나버립니다.

여러분 잠시 한번 눈을 지그시 감으시고 의식을 내면으로 돌리고 숨을 하단 깊은 곳으로 내려봅시다. 배꼽 아래 5cm 지점에 있는 하단의 깊은 곳에 집중해 보시기 바랍니다. 인체의 하단에는 우주의 엄청난 생명의 조화바다가 있습니다.

인류 원형 도통 수행에서 가장 중요한 게 호흡입니다. 우주와 소통하는 숨결이 중요합니다. 우선 눈을 지그시 감으시고 숨을 하단田丹으로 보냈다가 다시 머리 위 상단上丹으로 쭉 올려보세요. 그리고 다시 숨을 '후~' 하고 내쉬면서 쭉 배꼽 아래의 하단으로 내려보겠습니다. 이제 음악을 들으면서 집중해서 하단과 상단을 왔다갔다 하면서 호흡해 보겠습니다.

THE CORE OF HUMANITY'S ARCHETYPAL ENLIGHTENMENT MEDITATION

The energy of everyone who has gathered here today in Daegu is so nice and bright. It is a pleasure to meet you all.

The most precious place for the life of us humans—for our life force—is the lower *danjeon*. This is true because the lower *danjeon*'s essence is the source of energy for our body's life force. If this mysterious energy is depleted in our body, everything is finished.

Let's close our eyes for a moment, turn our consciousness inward, and inhale deeply into the depths of our lower *danjeon*. Please focus on the depths of your lower *danjeon*, which is five centimeters below your navel. Within the lower *danjeon* of the human body is an enormous cosmic sea of your life force's creation-transformation.

Breathing is the most important aspect of humanity's archetypal enlightenment meditation practices. Breathing to become one with the universe is crucial. First, close your eyes gently, and as you breathe, pull your energy down into your lower *danjeon*, and then raise your energy to the upper *danjeon* inside your forehead. In other words, as you exhale, send your energy down to the lower *danjeon* below your navel, and as you inhale, send your energy up to your upper *danjeon*. Now, while listening to calming music, let's breathe and send our energy back and forth between the lower *danjeon* and the upper *danjeon*.

31

하단은 우주의 조화바다의 세계이고, 상단은 우주의 무궁한 신의 세계입니다. 동방 우주관에서는 '하단을 본래 태수太水의 세계다. 물의 나라. 용궁龍宮이다'라고 했습니다. 신도로 보면 태수의 세계에 용이 깃들어 있습니다. 그리고 상단은 태화太火의 세계이며 불의 나라이며, 신도로 보면 불새, 봉황이 깃들어 있습니다. 그래서 우리 몸을 호흡으로 조율하면서 수행에 집중하면 몸 속 태수와 태화가 순환합니다. 영적으로는 용과 봉황이 순환하는 것입니다.

환국과 배달과 단군조선 시대의 어린이들은 동방원형 삼신수행법으로 하단의 물의 나라, 상단의 불의 나라의 기운을 순환시켰습니다. 그때는 몸속 달과 태양을 순환시켜 조화롭고 건강한 몸을 만들고, 대자연大自然과 소통했었습니다.

실제로 수행을 해보면 몸속에서 하단에 정精이 굳어져서 정단이 형성되면서 알이 생성됩니다. 그리고 알이 깨어지면서 불새, 즉 봉황이 나오면서 상단으로 올라갑니다. 그리고 상단의 용이 내려오면서 수승화강水昇火降의 조화가 몸속에서 실제로 이뤄지는 것입니다.

지금도 많은 도생이 몸속에서 정단형성이 되고, 용과 봉황이 순환하는 조화로운 경계를 체험하고 있습니다.

The lower *danjeon* is the cosmic realm of the sea of creation-transformation, and the upper *danjeon* is the infinite spirit realm. In Eastern cosmology, it was once said that the lower *danjeon* is the original realm of Great Water. It is a realm of water energy. It is the Dragon Palace in our body. Through your spiritual eye, you will see a dragon residing within this realm of Great Water. Meanwhile, the upper *danjeon* is the realm of Great Fire—a realm of fire. Through your spiritual eye, you will also see a fire bird—a phoenix—residing within. So when you are deeply focused on breathing meditation, the Great Water and Great Fire within will circulate. In a spiritual sense, this means the dragon and phoenix circulate.

In the eras of Hwanguk, Baedal, and Dangun Joseon, even children circulated the energy of the lower *danjeon*'s water realm and the upper *danjeon*'s fire realm by practicing archetypal Samsin meditation. Back then, they cultivated harmonious and healthy bodies and achieved communion with Mother Nature by circulating the moon and sun within.

True meditation concentrates the essence within the body's lower *danjeon*, forming the essence orb of light, which looks like an egg. When the egg hatches, a fire bird—the phoenix—emerges and ascends to the upper *danjeon*. And as the dragon of the upper *danjeon* descends, the harmony of 'ascending water, descending fire' is achieved in the body.

Even now there are many dao practitioners who have created an essence orb of light within their bodies and are directly experiencing the harmonious realm created as the dragon and phoenix circulate.

신선문명의 뿌리, 마고 할머니 문화

2만 5천 년 전에 우주 창조의 빛의 파장이자 모든 소리의 원형을 '옴'으로 가져오셔서 인간의 몸을 빛의 몸으로 전환하는 조화신선 도통법을 처음 전수하신 분이 마고성 율국시대의 마고할머니입니다.

한마디로 마고 삼신할머니는 인류 조화신선문명의 근원 되시는 분입니다. 아주 높으신 분입니다. 그래서 그 누구도 이분 앞에서는 아주 쩔쩔맵니다. 어떤 부처도, 어떤 성자도, 어떤 역사 속 영웅도 이분 앞에서는 감히 고개를 들지 못합니다.

마고 삼신할머니는 생로병사의 힘겨운 삶을 살 수밖에 없는 인간을 가엾게 보시고 '내가 쇠병사장을 뿌리 뽑겠다' 해서 웅대한 전략을 짜셨습니다.

그래서 마고 삼신할머니가 3천 년 동안 빈틈없이 설계를 해서 대우주의 영원하신 본체삼신이신 태허령님께 가서 '내가 인간을 신선으로 만들 계획이 있으니 손가락을 겁시다.'라고 약속해서 이 계획이 실행되게 된 것입니다. 태허령님은 우주의 본체신으로 꽉 찬 빛의 존재이십니다.

GRANDMOTHER MAGO: THE ROOT OF THE CIVILIZATION OF IMMORTALITY

Grandmother Mago of the Mago Castle of the Yulguk era was the first one to teach the immortality enlightenment meditation required for humans to attain a body of light. She did this twenty-five thousand years ago by bringing to earth the light waves of cosmic creation and all original sounds, condensing them all within the sound *om*.

In short, Grandmother Mago was the source of humanity's civilization of immortality. She was a sublimely exalted being. Anyone, no matter who they were, felt humble in her presence. No buddha, saint, or hero in history dared hold their head up before her.

Grandmother Mago took pity on humans, who had no choice but to endure the difficult process of life. She devised a grand strategy, saying, "I will extract the very roots of aging, illness, and death to eliminate them from this world."

So, Grandmother Mago designed a seamless blueprint over a period of three thousand years and then went to the Holy Spirit of Great Emptiness, the principal of the Primal Samsin of the universe, and made an offer: "I have a plan to make humans immortals. Let's do it together." And so, after they agreed to work together, the plan was put into action. As the Primal Spirit of the cosmos, the Holy Spirit of Great Emptiness was a being completely

마고 삼신할머니가 우주의 영원한 조화의 근원에 있는 모든 기운과 빛의 파동과 에너지를 모아서 인간문명의 소리로 내려주셨습니다. 다시 말해, 우주의 시공간을 낳은 근원의 조화 생명인 '옴' 소리를 뭉쳐서 인류가 신선이 되는 길을 처음 열어주신 분이십니다.

그래서 태허령님은 '내가 마고 삼신할머니한테 코를 꿨다.'고 하십니다. 이건 동방 전통의 도통세계에서 내려오는 말씀입니다. 어떤 문서에도 없고, 여기에서만 들을 수 있는 겁니다. 조화도통의 아주 깊고 깊은 신선세계에서 내려오는 은밀한 일화입니다.

suffused with light.

Grandmother Mago brought together all the energy and waves of light present in the source of the eternal creation-transformation of the cosmos and transformed them into a sound, which was bestowed upon human civilization. In other words, she was the first to open the way for humankind to become immortals by condensing this energy and light into the sound *om*, the fundamental life force that gave birth to time and space in the universe.

Regarding this, the Holy Spirit of Great Emptiness said, "Grandmother Mago won me over with her plan." This is a story passed down orally in the traditional Eastern world of enlightenment. Not recorded in any book, the story is something you won't hear anywhere else but here in Jeung San Do. It is a secret tale passed down from a very deep realm of immortality enlightenment.

새로운 문명을 여는 삼신 조화도통 수행법

진정 인류의 새로운 문명을 열 수 있는 동력은 무엇일까요? AI, 첨단 로봇의 힘을 빌어서 인류가 안고 있는 문제점이 해결될 수 있을까요?

그런데 인간 삶의 바탕인 대자연이 병들었고, 그로 인해 인간 몸이 병들어가는데 기계문명만으로 모든 게 해결되는 게 아니라는 것입니다. 상제님은 '하늘과 땅이 병들었기에 그것을 뜯어고쳐야 인간이 살 수 있다'고 하셨습니다.

그래서 우리의 몸과 마음을 원천적으로 새롭게 할 수 있는 도통道通만이 진정으로 새문명을 열 수 있는 동력원이 됩니다. 물론 기계문명의 도움을 받지만 근원은 인간에게 있는 것입니다.

지금은 생존生存 수행해야 합니다. 도통만이 진정으로 인간 문명을 새롭게 할 수 있습니다. 우리 한사람 한사람이 소중한 우주의 중심체, 우주의 본체입니다. 그러니 우리 스스로가 내 몸과 마음과 영체를 완전히 변화시키면서 어둠을 몰아내고, 온갖 피로한 기운과 좌절, 트라우마와 슬픔 등을 완전히 몰아내면서 우주의 근원,

GIVING BIRTH TO A NEW CIVILIZATION: SAMSIN MEDITATION FOR ENLIGHTENMENT

What is the true driving force that will enable a new civilization for humankind? Can we use AI and the power of cutting-edge robots to solve the problems of humankind?

Since sickness is afflicting nature, the basis of human life, our human bodies have also become ill. This shows that a civilization based solely on machines cannot solve everything. Sangjenim taught that heaven and earth are sick, and humans will only be able to survive if heaven and earth are healed.

Moreover, only enlightenment that can fundamentally renew our bodies and minds will adequately serve as a genuine driving force to establish a new civilization. Of course, humans will use the assistance of machines, but the impetus will always rest with humans.

Now is the time that we must practice meditation for self-preservation and survival. Only enlightenment can truly transform human civilization into something new. Each individual human being is a precious embodiment of the universe. Therefore, we must be one with the source of the universe, the infinite light of the absolute realm of the cosmic life force. We can do so by completely transforming our bodies, minds, and souls as we drive out all darkness, spent energy, frustration, trauma,

우주생명의 절대 세계의 무궁한 빛과 하나돼야 합니다. 한마디로 우리 몸과 마음을 광명의 빛으로 채우는 끊임없는 과정이 절대적으로 필요합니다. 그게 삼신조화 수행법입니다.

and sadness. In short, we implicitly require an enduring process that will fill our bodies and minds with the light of radiance. This process is Samsin meditation.

'나'라는 존재를 완성시키는 수행

수행이란 무엇일까요? 왜 우리는 수행을 해야 할까요? 한마디로 수행을 해야 우리 인간 존재에 대한 갈증이 해소되기 때문입니다. 천지에서 생명을 받아 태어난 인간은 수행을 하지 않으면 충족되지 않는 그 무엇이 있습니다.

현대인들은 '돈만 있으면 만사 오케이'라는 말을 자주 합니다. 그런데 그것만 가지고 해결되지 않는 문제가 있는 겁니다. 노쇠하고 병들어가시는 부모님의 모습, 또 이웃들과 가족들이 코로나에 걸려서 힘겨워하는 것을 보며 '인생이란 무엇인지'를 되묻지 않을 수가 없는 겁니다.

지금 지구촌의 생태학자들은 '지구촌의 환경이 병들어서 크고 작은 정말로 무서운 병들이 끊임없이 닥쳐온다.'고 경고합니다. 지구환경이 얼마나 무섭게 무너지고 있습니까? 생명의 어머니 지구의 시스템이 무너져서 혹한과 혹서 등의 여러 문제가 생기고, 그 속에서 온갖 질병이 몰려오고 있는 겁니다. 지금 인류는 지구 환경의 임계점, 임팩트 존을 통과하며 낭떠러지를 향해서 걸어가고 있는 것입니다.

MEDITATION BRINGS FULFILLMENT TO OUR HUMAN EXISTENCE

What is meditation? Why must we meditate? In short, we must meditate because meditation is the only way to quench the thirst of our human existence. Since humans are born into this world by receiving life from heaven and earth, we are unfulfilled unless we meditate.

People often say, "Everything is okay as long as you have money." However, there are deeper problems that cannot be solved simply with money. One can't help but ask what the value of life is when they see their aging and sick parents, or their neighbors and family members, suffering after catching illnesses such as COVID-19.

Meanwhile, ecologists around the world are sounding the alarm about the grave illness afflicting the global environment, and the minor, major, and truly frightening diseases that are constantly appearing. Just how frightening is this global environmental collapse? The systems of earth, the mother of all life, are failing. This is causing various problems, such as extremely cold or hot temperatures, and all kinds of diseases are arising as a result. Humans are now moving past the point of no return—the tipping point for the global environment—toward a cliff.

『THE SONG OF THE CELL ^{세포들의 노래}』의 놀라운 메시지

지금 인류에게 닥친 지구환경의 한계 속에서 파생된 생명과 죽음의 문제는 그 무엇으로도 극복할 수 없습니다. 금년에 나온 세계적인 히트작인 『THE SONG OF THE CELL』라는 책이 있는데 이틀 전에 받아서 보니깐 놀라운 이야기를 합니다.

'세포에도 세포 공동체가 있다. 여러 가지의 세포가 함께 하나의 사회처럼 조율됨으로써 우리 몸의 건강과 정서와 평화로움이 확보된'는 겁니다. 우리 몸의 세포들이 노래를 하는 겁니다. 세포단위에서 우리들이 누구를 미워하고 화를 내는지, 누구를 진실한 마음으로 사랑하는지 까지를 정확하게 안다는 겁니다.

그래서 우리가 수행할 때도 온몸의 세포들이 다함께 진동을 하는 겁니다. 상제님께서도 '네 몸에 있는 세포들이 대우주와 하나되는 순간이 있다. 궁극 깨달음의 도통주문인 시천주주와 태을주를 한마음으로 노래할 때 그 순간부터 네가 온 우주와 소통이 된'고 말씀하셨습니다. 수행자가 다른 생각을 하고 고민을 하면 우

44

THE AMAZING MESSAGE IN
The Song of the Cell

There is no way present-day humankind can overcome this life-or-death crisis stemming from global environmental limitations. There was a book released last year called *The Song of the Cell* that became an international bestseller. I got it two days ago, and it has an amazing story to tell.

The book says that even cells have their own communities. When the various cells coordinate together like a society, your physical and emotional well-being and general tranquility are ensured. The cells in our bodies sing. At the cellular level, we know precisely who we hate, who angers us, and who we love with a true heart.

That's why cells throughout your body vibrate together when you meditate. Sangjenim also said that there is a moment when the cells in your body become one with the universe. You enter into communication with the entire cosmos the moment you chant the Sicheonjuju and Taeeulju mantras—the mantras of ultimate enlightenment—with one mind. However, if a meditator is thinking or worrying about anything, how could they possibly communicate with the universe, maintain a state of one mind, and achieve enlightenment?

The Song of the Cell contains much content that will foster a new awakening. Please keep in mind that when

주와 소통이 되고, 한마음을 갖고 도통을 할 수 있겠느냐는 말씀입니다.

『THE SONG OF THE CELL』에는 새롭게 각성할 수 있는 많은 내용이 담겨 있습니다. '내 몸속에 있는 수억 조의 세포들이 한마음이 될 때 우리가 대우주와 하나가 될 수 있는 진정한 깨달음의 존재가 된다'는 것을 명심하시기 바랍니다.

the trillions of cells in your body become one, you will develop into a truly enlightened being who is one with the cosmos.

우주의 소리, 빛, 꽃

  마고할머니께서 '우주에는 원음^{原音}이 있다. 우주의 심장에서 울려오는 영원한 생명의 소리인 율려^{律呂}가 있다'고 하십니다. 율려는 음양의 언어로 여정^{呂靜}과 율동^{律動} 즉, 고요함과 동함을 상징합니다. 그런데 율동은 알지만 여정은 잘 모릅니다. 자연과 더불어 하나가 돼서 움직이는 율동과 진정한 고요함을 맛보는 여정을 다 체험할 때 인간은 완전한 존재가 되는 겁니다.

  그러나 우주의 음원인 옴과 훔 소리만을 갖고는 깨달음을 얻고 선체^{仙體(신선의 몸)}를 득하기 어려우니 선려화^{仙呂花}를 주신 것입니다. 즉, 우주의 율려소리, 율려조화의 빛을 우리 몸에다가 탁탁탁 붙여서 세포 단위까지 심을 수 있게 천상의 빛꽃, 우주 율려의 조화꽃, 천상의 신선꽃인 선려화를 내려주신 것입니다.

  선려화의 원 이름은 선정화^{仙定花}입니다. '신선 선^仙 자, 정할 정^定 자, 꽃 화^花 자'로 신선이 됨을 결정하는 조화꽃이라는 뜻입니다. 그런데 마고 할머께서 '기초 수행자 너희들은 아직 신선이 안 됐으니 꽃은 똑같은데 기능만 조금 다른 꽃을 내려준다. 이를 선려화라고 해

THE SOUND, LIGHT, AND FLOWERS OF THE COSMOS

Grandmother Mago said, "There is the original sound of the universe. There is *yullyeo*, the eternal sound of life that rings out from the heart of the cosmos." In terms of yin and yang, yullyeo represents both yeojeong ("stillness") and yuldong ("movement"). In other words, *yullyeo* entails both stillness and movement. Yet, while *yuldong* is a well-known term, many are not aware of the term *yeojeong*. Humans become complete beings when they experience: the *yuldong* of becoming one with nature and moving with nature; the *yeojeong* of tasting true stillness and tranquility.

However, it is hard to gain enlightenment and obtain the body of an immortal solely by mastering *om* and *hoom*, the original sounds of the universe. This is why Grandmother Mago also gave us the Seollyeohwa ("Flower of Immortality"). She bestowed upon us the Seollyeohwa—the heavenly flower of light, the creation-transformation flower of cosmic *yullyeo*, and the immortal flower of heaven—so that the cosmic sound of *yullyeo*, which contains the light of *yullyeo* creation-transformation, would be planted within our bodies even at the cellular level.

The original term for the Seollyeohwa was "Seonjeonghwa"—the "Immortality Decider Flower." Comprised of the characters *seon* ("immortality"), *jeong* ("decision"),

라' 해서 선려화라고 칭하게 된 것입니다.

2차 수행에 들어가면 선정화를 내려 받게 됩니다. 우주의 깊은 세계, 우주의 본체삼신이신 태허령太虛靈님의 무극無極 세계에 거대하고 하얀 꽃이 있습니다. 사람이 다섯 명 정도 앉을 수 있는 거대한 꽃인데요, 2차 수행을 통해서 내려받게 될 것입니다. 이 선정화를 내려받으면 우리 몸의 일곱 혈자리에 전부 꽃이 펴서 인간꽃이 되는 것입니다.

지금은 우선 선려화를 1차 수행을 통해 내려받고 몸에 심어서 아픈 곳을 치유하고 빛의 몸으로 바꿔나가야합니다. 그리고 선려화의 원형꽃, 어머니 꽃이라 할 수 있는 선정화를 받기 전에 150세의 수명줄을 내려받는수행도 하게 됩니다.

and *hwa* ("flower"), this term means the "flower that determines immortality." However, Grandmother Mago also said, "Because you beginner meditators have not yet become immortals, I will bestow upon you the exact same flower, but with a slightly different function. This, you should call the 'Seollyeohwa.'" With that, she gave the Seollyeohwa its name.

When one enters the second stage of meditation, they will receive the Seonjeonghwa. One who enters the depths of the universe will see a very large Seongjeonghwa. It is a giant white flower located in the Mugeuk realm of the Holy Spirit of Great Emptiness, the principal of the Primal Samsin of the cosmos. This giant flower is large enough for about five people to sit upon, and it will descend to you through the second stage of meditation. Then, when you receive the Seonjeonghwa, all seven of your energy centers will bloom with a flower and you yourself will become a human flower.

Now, your first task is to carry out the first stage of meditation to receive the Seollyeohwa, plant it in your body to heal all areas of pain, and attain a body of light. Then, you will enter a process of meditation for receiving a life span of 150 years prior to obtaining the Seonjeonghwa—the original Seollyeohwa that can also be referred to as the "Mother Flower."

侍天主呪

시 천 주 주

The Sicheonjuju Mantra

太乙呪

태 을 주

The Taeeulju Mantra

侍天主造化定 永世不忘萬事知 至氣今至願爲大降

시천주조화정 영세불망만사지 지기금지원위대강

Si cheon ju Jo hwa jeong Yeong se bul mang man sa ji Ji gi geum ji won wi dae gang

吽哆 吽哆 太乙天上元君 吽哩哆哪都来 吽哩喊哩娑婆訶

흠치 흠치 태을천상원군 흠리치야도래 흠리함리사파하

Hoom chi Hoom chi Tae eul cheon Sang won gun Hoom ri chi ya do rae Hoom ri ham ri sa pa ha

66

You can enter into communication
with the entire cosmos the moment
you chant the Sicheonjuju and Taeeulju
mantras—the mantras of ultimate
enlightenment—with one mind.

99

동방 1만 년 신교문화의 부활
동학과 참동학

Eastern Learning and True Eastern Learning:

The Revival of the East's Ten-Thousand-Year Culture of Spirit Teaching

동방신선학교

오늘, 이곳 대구에서 역사적인 '동방신선학교 출범'을 선언합니다. 그리고 이틀 후 월요일 저녁부터 동방신선학교 1기가 본격적으로 시작됩니다. 이 자리에 오신 여러분을 비롯한 지구촌 어느 누구에게도 문을 활짝 열어놓으니까 다 들어오실 수 있습니다. 코로나19로 신음呻吟하는 대한민국의 국민들과 지구촌 형제자매들의 건강을 위해서 발족하는 것입니다.

동방신선학교는 지구촌 인류가 삼신상제님의 조화법을 받아 병란의 파도를 넘어 능히 선체가 될 수 있는 유일한 새로운 희망의 장이 될 것입니다. 내 몸과 마음과 영체 속 일체의 어둠을 몰아내고 150세 수명줄을 받아서 무병장수할 수 있는 신선의 길을 밟아가게 될 것입니다.

1차로 자신부터 체험하시고, '소중한 부모, 형제, 아내와 남편, 자녀들에게 같이 하자, 아주 즐겁고 좋다'고 해서 함께 하시기 바랍니다. 선려화를 받고 수행을 통해 치병한 사례를 들어보면 정말로 감동적이고 놀라운 체험들이 많습니다.

THE EASTERN SCHOOL OF IMMORTALITY MEDITATION

Today, here in Daegu, we are announcing the historic launch of the Eastern School of Immortality Meditation. And two days from now, the first Eastern School of Immortality Meditation will begin in earnest on Monday evening. Its doors are wide open to anyone around the world, including you who have come here today. Everyone is welcome. We launched this school for the health of the Korean people and of our global brothers and sisters after much suffering due to COVID-19.

The Eastern School of Immortality Meditation will be a place of hope, where the world's people will receive teachings of Samsin Sangjenim's principle of creation-transformation to overcome disasters of disease and attain bodies of immortality. You will walk the path of becoming an immortal by expelling all the darkness from your body, mind, and soul and receiving a 150-year life span that will enable you to attain eternal health and longevity.

I hope you all will begin by trying the first stage of meditation for yourselves and then tell your precious parents, siblings, wives, husbands, and children how enjoyable and beneficial it is so that you and they might practice it together. As you continue your practice, you'll also be inspired by the stories of those who were healed through Seollyeohwa meditation, where you'll encounter

한 구도자의 예를 들면 눈의 망막이 출혈이 되고 안 뵈는데 병원에서도 '수술해서 잘못하면 실명도 할 수 있다'고 할 정도로 심각한데요, 스스로 자각해서 선려화를 심고서 정성껏 수행하니 아픈 게 싹 사라지고 앞이 보이더라는 이야기를 합니다.

이것은 우주의 조화법, 놀라운 조화 도통법을 쓰는 것입니다. 이게 인류의 원형문화입니다. 환국과 배달국, 조선 시대의 수행법입니다.

truly moving and amazing experiences.

One male seeker, for example, had bleeding in the retina of his eye and couldn't see as a result. Even the hospital said, "If the surgery goes wrong, you could lose your eyesight permanently." So, after this dao seeker had a personal awakening, he engaged in sincere meditation and planted Seollyeohwa flowers within his eye. The pain then disappeared completely, and he was able to see.

This was done by using cosmic immortality enlightenment meditation—the amazing meditation practice for enlightenment. This was at the heart of the archetypal culture of humanity. This was the meditation method used during the Hwanguk, Baedal, and Dangun Joseon eras.

신교문화의 부활을 알린
동학의 3대 메시지

19세기 동학을 통해 환국과 배달과 단군조선의 신교
神敎문화가 부활했습니다. 동학은 '동방에서 배운다.'는
뜻입니다. 동학을 알아야 동방의 진정한 원형문화를 아
는 겁니다.

그럼 동학의 창시자 최수운 대신사께서 주장하신 세
가지의 핵심 주제는 무엇일까요? 우리가 300만 동학혁
명의 꿈과 대이상을 성취하기 위해서라도 이것을 제대
로 알아야 합니다.

첫째, '다시 개벽'이 온다는 것입니다. 우주의 섭리로
개벽이 다시 닥친다는 것입니다. 둘째, 시천주 메시지
입니다. 우주의 통치자이신 아버지를 모시는 때가 되었
다는 것입니다. 셋째, 아버지의 도법인 무극대도가 나
온다는 것입니다. 무극대도는 아버지의 도법이자, 인류
문명을 새롭게 할 조화법입니다.

그리고 결론적으로 최수운 대신사는 돌아가시기 전
에 '우주의 아버지가 자신이 이 세상을 떠난 뒤 8년 후
에 조선 땅에 강세하신다'고 선언했습니다.

THREE CORE MESSAGES OF EASTERN LEARNING THAT ANNOUNCED THE REVIVAL OF SPIRIT TEACHING CULTURE

The Spirit Teaching culture of Hwanguk, Baedal, and Dangun Joseon was revived by Eastern Learning in the nineteenth century. The original Korean name for Eastern Learning is 'Donghak,' which means "Teachings of the East." Understanding Eastern Learning is the key to understanding the true archetypal culture of the East.

So, what were the three core teachings asserted by Great Divine Teacher Choe Su-un, the founder of Eastern Learning? We need to have a proper grasp of them in order for us to achieve the dreams and grand ideals of the three-million-strong Eastern Learning Revolution.

The first core teaching is that *gaebyeok* is coming again. This means it is cosmic providence that another *gaebyeok* is impending. The second core teaching is the message of *sicheonju* ("serving the Lord of Heaven"). This means that the time has come to serve the Heavenly Father, Ruler of the Universe. The third core teaching is that the Supreme Dao of Mugeuk, the dao of the Father, is coming to the fore. The Supreme Dao of Mugeuk is the dao of the Father underpinning the enlightenment meditation that will renew human civilization.

In addition, before passing away, Great Divine Teacher Choe Su-un proclaimed that, eight years after his own death, the Father of the Universe would incarnate into

한마디로 '천상의 아버지가 오신다. 공자, 석가, 예수를 내려보내시고 하늘과 땅, 인간계와 신계를 다스리시는 우주의 아버지가 이 땅에 오신다'는 겁니다.

이것을 노래한 것이 시천주주侍天主呪입니다. '시천주조화정 영세불망만사지' 열석 자 주문입니다. 최수운 대신사는 '열석 자 지극하면 만권시서 무엇하리'라고도 했습니다. 천하의 모든 지식보다 천주님을 몸에 모시고 조화를 받는 것이 중요하다는 의미입니다.

this world. He said, "The Heavenly Father is coming. The Father of the Universe—who sent to us Confucius, Shakyamuni, and Jesus and who rules heaven, earth, and the human and spirit realms—will come to this land."

This is sung about in the Sicheonjuju Mantra. The Sicheonjuju Mantra is a mantra of thirteen words: "*Si-cheon-ju Jo-hwa-jeong, Yeong-se-bul-mang-man-sa-ji*" ("Serving the Lord of Heaven, I determine the destiny of the Immortal Paradise of Creation-Transformation. I will never forget, throughout all eternity, his infinite grace of bestowing enlightenment into all matters"). Great Divine Teacher Choe Su-un also said, "If you chant the thirteen words with utmost devotion, what need will you have of ten thousand scriptures?" This means that serving the Lord of Heaven and receiving his creation-transformation is more important than all knowledge produced on earth.

시천주 주문의 원뜻과 상제님 강세

시천주 주문은 누구를 모시는 주문일까요? 한마디로 천지의 원주인이신 천주天主님입니다. 천주 아버지를 모시는 주문입니다.

그런데 천주의 다른 말이 상제上帝님입니다. 그래서 우리가 시천주 주문을 송주한다는 것은 '천주 아버지이신 상제님을 모시고 조화세계, 조화신선문명을 결정짓는다'는 것입니다. 여기서 모실 시侍 자와 정할 정定 자가 중요합니다. 바로 천주님을 모셔야 조화가 정해진다는 것입니다.

상제님께서는 최수운 대신사에게 시천주 주문을 내려주실 때 '시천주 조화정'을 글자로 써서 내려주셨는데 그중에서 '시侍' 자와 '정定' 자를 아주 크게 쓰셨습니다. 그리고 나머지 '영세불망만사지 지기금지원위대강'은 직접 소리 내어 읽어서 내려주셨습니다.

이 사실은 동학하는 사람도 잘 모릅니다. 우리가 직접 시천주 주문을 사무치게 많이 읽어서 상제님과 교감이 되어야 아는 세계입니다.

동학의 선언은 시천주侍天主 조화정造化定입니다. 천주

The Meaning of the Sicheonjuju Mantra; Sangjenim's Human Incarnation

The Sicheonjuju Mantra focuses on serving a supreme being, but who is this being? That supreme being is the Lord of Heaven, the original master of heaven and earth. And so, the Sicheonjuju Mantra is the mantra about serving the Heavenly Father, the Lord of Heaven.

Another name for the Lord of Heaven is 'Sangje.' So, the Sicheonjuju Mantra signifies that we serve the Lord of Heaven, the Heavenly Father Sangjenim, and establish the realm of creation-transformation—the civilization of immortality. Here, the characters *si* ("to serve") and *jeong* ("to decide") are important. Together, they mean that you must serve the Lord of Heaven to establish the realm of creation-transformation.

When Sangjenim bestowed the Sicheonjuju Mantra upon Great Divine Teacher Choe Su-un, Sangjenim presented to Su-un the first part of the mantra in writing—'*Si-cheon-ju Jo-hwa-jeong*'—with the words *si* and *jeong* appearing much larger than the rest. Sangjenim then presented the rest of the mantra by chanting it: "*Yeong-se-bul-mang-man-sa-ji Ji-gi-geum-ji-won-wi-dae-gang.*"

Even practitioners of Eastern Learning were unaware of this fact. The inner meaning of the Sicheonjuju Mantra can only be understood by sincerely chanting the mantra countless times and communicating with Sangjenim.

님을 모시고 조화를 정한다는 것입니다. 최수운의 선언 그대로 8년 후인 1871년 신미년에 이 땅에 천주님이 강세하셨습니다.

『도전』을 보면 놀라운 말씀이 있습니다.

"예수를 믿는 사람은 예수의 재림을 기다리고 불교도는 미륵의 출세를 기다리고 동학 신도는 최수운의 갱생을 기다리나니 '누구든지 한 사람만 오면 각기 저의 스승이라.' 하여 따르리라. '예수가 재림한다.' 하나 곧 나를 두고 한 말이니라. 공자, 석가, 예수는 내가 쓰기 위해 내려 보냈느니라."(道典 2:40)

인간으로 오신 강증산 상제님이 바로 공자, 석가, 예수, 최수운을 쓰기 위해 내려보냈다는 것입니다. 그런데 서교에서는 아버지를 찾지 못하고 '재림 예수'만 찾고 있습니다. 예수가 올 날만 학수고대하고 있는 것입니다. 그런데 서교의 경전을 보면, 예수는 아버지를 찾습니다. 아버지가 자신을 보내서 왔다고 역사의 진실을 말합니다. 그리고 12 사도 중의 한 사람인 사도 요한은 백보좌에 계신 아버지 하느님을 뵙게 됩니다. 성서의 마지막인 『요한계시록』을 보십시오. 그때 백보좌의 아버지는 "나는 알파와 오메가라 이제도 있고 전에도 있

Eastern Learning's proclamation was "*si-cheon-ju jo-hwa-jeong.*" This means, "serving the Lord of Heaven, I determine the destiny of the Immortal Paradise of Creation-Transformation." Eight years later, in 1871, the Lord of Heaven incarnated in this land, just as Choe Su-un had foretold.

The Dojeon contains an amazing teaching:

> Those who believe in Jesus await the second coming of Jesus, those who believe in Buddha await the coming of Maitreya Buddha, and those who believe in Eastern Learning await the re-birth of Choe Su-un. But whoever this person proves to be, when that one person comes, all will proclaim him their master and follow him. They say "Jesus will come again," but these words actually signify my arrival. I sent Confucius, Shakyamuni, and Jesus to the world, to serve in my work.
> (Sangjenim, Dojeon, 2:40)

Before incarnating into this world, Gahng Jeung-san Sangjenim sent down Confucius, Shakyamuni, Jesus, and Choe Su-un to earth to employ them in his work. However, the Father is lost to adherents of Christianity, who merely await the return of Jesus. They do nothing more than eagerly wait for the day Jesus will return. And yet, the scripture of this Western theology—Christianity—shows that Jesus himself sought the Father. He speaks a historical truth within it, saying that it was the Father who sent him. And one of the twelve apostles, John, saw

었고 '장차 올 자'요 전능한 자라."^(요한계시록 1:8)라고 선언하고 있습니다.

태라천太羅天에 계신 아버지 상제님께서 예수의 12사도 중에 가장 잘 믿고 기도를 잘하는 사도요한을 천상으로 올라오게 하신 겁니다. 그때 아버지 상제님은 '태라천궁의 작은 성전에서 내가 요한에게 앞으로 새우주가 열리는 걸 보여줬다'라고 하십니다. 그게 『요한계시록』입니다.

그래서 계시록을 보면 요한이 "나는 보았습니다. 새하늘, 새 땅을 보았습니다. 예전의 하늘과 땅은 다시 있지 않았습니다."^(요한계시록 21)라고 했습니다. 완전히 새로운 우주가 열리는 것을 본 것입니다.

그럼 동학과 서교의 결론은 무엇입니까? 지금은 아버지 상제님을 모시고 조화를 정하는 때요, 새하늘과 새땅이 열리는 '다시 개벽'의 때라는 것입니다. 새로운 우주의 탄생 속에서 인류도 새롭게 되라는 겁니다. 이제 백보좌 하느님이신 상제님의 삼신조화 도통수행법으로 인류는 진정 새로운 생명으로, 빛의 인간으로 태어나는 엄청난 기적의 새로운 역사를 활짝 펼치게 됩니다.

God the Father sitting on his white throne. Look at Revelation, by John, at the end of the New Testament, which says that the Father on the white throne proclaimed to John:

> I am the Alpha and the Omega… who is, and who was, and who is to come, the Almighty. (Revelation 1:8).

Sangjenim, the Father who resides in Taeracheon Heaven, summoned to heaven John, the one among the twelve disciples of Jesus who prayed the most sincerely. Father Sangjenim said of that time: "Within a small temple of the Taeracheon Heaven Palace, I revealed to John a vision of the new universe to come." This is what was described in Revelation.

This is why John said in Revelation, "Then I saw a new heaven and a new earth, for the first heaven and the first earth had passed away…" (Revelation 21). He had seen the birth of a completely new cosmos.

Then, what is the ultimate message of Eastern Learning and Western theology? It is this: now is the time to serve Father Sangjenim and establish creation-transformation, for the time of *gaebyeok* has again come to create a new heaven and earth. And, amid the birth of a new cosmos, humanity will be renewed. Now, with the Samsin meditation practice of Sangjenim, a new miraculous history will unfold in which humans are truly reborn with new life as humans of light.

이제 아버지 상제님의
무극대도 조화법이 나와야

조금 전에 살펴본 동학의 핵심은 다시 개벽과 시천주侍天主와 무극대도無極大道의 도래입니다. 이제 우주의 섭리로 다시 개벽의 때가 닥친다. 이를 위해 천주 아버지, 상제님께서 인간으로 오신다. 그리고 아버지의 도법인 무극대도가 나온다는 것입니다. 이렇게 간명하게 동학의 핵심이 정리되지만 안타깝게도 기존의 동학 책들은 제대로 정의를 못 하고 있습니다. 그래서 여러분이 책을 읽어도 제대로 된 동학의 본질을 모르는 겁니다.

그럼 무극대도無極大道란 무엇일까요?

무극대도는 무극삼신의 조화법입니다. 우주의 깊고 깊은 무극세계에는 본체삼신이신 태허령님과 태성령님과 태광령님이 계십니다. 삼신三神님의 세계는 무궁무궁한 빛의 세계, 무극의 세계입니다.

그리고 우주에 상제님이 계십니다. 우리 조상들은 상제님이 우주의 본체삼신님과 하나된 우주의 주재자임을 알았습니다. 그래서 상제님을 '삼신일체 상제님'이라고 칭했던 것입니다.

FATHER SANGJENIM'S ENLIGHTENMENT MEDITATION MUST NOW BE PRACTICED

As we just examined, the core messages of Eastern Learning were 'another *gaebyeok*,' *sicheonju* ("serving the Lord of Heaven"), and the advent of the Supreme Dao of Mugeuk. In other words, the providence of heaven dictates that another *gaebyeok* is impending. For this reason, Father Sangjenim, the Lord of Heaven, incarnated into this world; and the Supreme Dao of Mugeuk, the dao of the Father, will come forth. Although the core of Eastern Learning can be simply and clearly defined with these three messages, current Eastern Learning literature is unable to properly do so. This is why you all will have been unaware of the true essence of Eastern Learning.

But just what is the Supreme Dao of Mugeuk?

The Supreme Dao of Mugeuk is the creation-transformation principle of Mugeuk Samsin. In the realm of Mugeuk, in the deepest part of the universe, resides the Primal Samsin comprised of the Holy Spirit of Great Emptiness, the Holy Spirit of Great Holiness, and the Holy Spirit of Great Radiance. The realm of Samsin is the realm of infinite light—the realm of Mugeuk.

In the cosmic realm resides Sangjenim. Our ancestors knew Sangjenim to be the Ruler of the Universe, who is one with the Primal Samsin. That is why they called him "Sangjenim Who Is One with Samsin."

이제 무극의 조화기운을 한없이 주시는 아버지 상제님의 조화 신선도통법이 나온다는 것이 동학의 무극대도 선언입니다. 본체삼신님과 상제님이 하나 돼서 인류 문명을 새롭게 바꿔 놓으시는 것입니다.

동학의 최수운 대신사는 '무극대도 닦아내니 5만 년 운수로다'(『용담유사』「안심가」)라고 하셨습니다. 앞으로 인간 농사 짓는 우주1년에서 후천 5만년 세상이 남았습니다. 상제님의 조화문화, 빛의 문화로 인류사가 거듭나게 됩니다. 그러면서 우주의 시공간이 새롭게 열리게 됩니다. 그것이 '다시 개벽'입니다.

최수운 대신사는 '12제국 괴질운수 다시 개벽 아닐런가'라고 했습니다. 인류가 괴질이 닥치는 운수를 만난다. 다시 개벽이 있다는 것을 전했습니다.

Eastern Learning's Supreme Dao of Mugeuk proclamation asserts that now is the time when Father Sangjenim's meditation for attaining immortality must be enacted to infinitely spread the creation-transformation energy of Mugeuk. This means that the Primal Samsin and Sangjenim will unite as one and transform human civilization.

Great Divine Teacher Choe Su-un of Eastern Learning said, "Cultivate and purify yourself with the Supreme Dao of Mugeuk and the destiny of the next fifty thousand years will be yours" ("Ansimga," *Yongdamyusa*). In this current cosmic year of human cultivation, the fifty thousand years of the Later Heaven still remain. Human history is about to be reborn in the form of Sangjenim's creation-transformation culture—the culture of light. Cosmic time and space will also be reestablished in this process. This is what is meant by the proclamation about another *gaebyeok*.

Great Divine Teacher Choe Su-un also said, "The fate of the mysterious disease spreading across the entire world—is this not once again *gaebyeok*?" He said that humanity is fated to be afflicted with a mysterious disease. He also taught that another *gaebyeok* is coming.

참동학 증산도의
의원도수와 만국의원도수

　동학의 300만 구도자 가운데 수많은 이들이 일제에 의해 참혹하게 멸망당했습니다. 그리고 살아남은 많은 구도자들은 8년 뒤에 이 땅에 오신 삼신상제님이신 증산 상제님의 도문에 들어가게 됩니다.

　증산 상제님을 모신 도문에 동학을 믿다가 찾아온 구도자들이 많았습니다. 차경석, 박공우, 문공신 등 많은 주요 성도들이 모두 동학교도였습니다.

　그럼 왜 상제님은 전라도 고부 땅에 강세하셨을까요? 이곳은 간방艮方 한반도에서도 삼신산三神山이 있는 곳입니다. 그 삼신산의 기운을 받는 마지막 자락인 고부군 우덕면 객망리의 시루산 아래에 강씨 성으로 상제님께서 오신 것입니다.

　『도전』을 읽어보십시오. 우주의 아버지가 강세하시어 '내가 이제 하늘도 뜯어고치고, 땅도 뜯어고쳐 물샐 틈없이 도수를 짜 놓았느니라'하시며 천지공사天地公事를 보셨습니다. 하늘과 땅을 새롭게 고치실 분은 천지의

'THE HEALER DOSU' AND 'THE DOSU OF THE CENTER FOR THE HEALING AND SAVING OF ALL NATIONS' OF JEUNG SAN DO

Hundreds of thousands of Eastern Learning's three million dao seekers were brutally wiped out by imperial Japan. And many of the surviving members of Eastern Learning later entered the dao order of Jeung-san Sangjenim, the human incarnation of Samsin Sangjenim.

These many seekers of dao turned to the dao order that served Jeung-san Sangjenim after once believing in Eastern Learning. A significant number of Sangjenim's main disciples—such as Cha Gyeong-seok, Bak Gong-u, and Mun Gong-sin—were among these former adherents of Eastern Learning.

But why did Sangjenim incarnate in Gobu of Jeolla-do Province? He did so because that area has the Samsin mountains—the three mountains possessing the greatest of affinities with Samsin, even when compared to the rest of the mountains of the Korean Peninsula, which itself is auspiciously located in the northeast. Sangjenim incarnated with the surname 'Gahng' at the foot of Sirusan Mountain, the last offshoot of a chain of mountains that receive the energy of Samsin. This mountain is located near Gaengmang-ri Village, Udeok-myeon Township, in Gobu County.

Please read about this in the Dojeon. The Father of the

원주인밖에 없습니다. 아버지 상제님은 병든 천지 간의 모든 병을 고치시는 대의왕大醫王입니다.

일차적으로 자연과 문명의 '다시 개벽'의 법도로 병란病亂이 몰려옵니다. 이 세상의 진정한 주제가 의원醫院 도수입니다. 크고 작은 병란이 태풍처럼 몰려오기 때문에 우선 각자 생존生存을 위해서 의원도수를 실천해야 합니다. 그리고 나아가 내 가족과 이웃, 천하창생을 건지는 만국萬國의원醫院도수가 발동되게 됩니다.

우리가 의원도수와 만국의원도수를 성취하는 과정에서 신선으로 거듭나게 됩니다. 상제님께서는 의원도수에 신선神仙도수와 갱소년更少年도수를 붙이셨습니다. 인류사의 총체적인 문제인 생로병사生老病死의 문제를 극복할 길을 열어주신 것입니다. 다시 10대의 건강한 몸으로 되돌아갈 길이 열린 것입니다.

그러나 쉽게 되지는 않고, 몇 십 년을 제대로 닦아야 합니다. 섭생을 잘하고 마음을 잘 먹고 수행도 잘해야 합니다.

우리가 2차 수행단계에 가면 내 몸의 유전자의 노화를 막고 다시 젊어질 수 있는 수행을 하게 됩니다. 일반적으로 시간은 현재에서 미래로 흘러갑니다. 그런데 시간을 주재하시는 태광령太光靈님의 옥좌에 가면 그분의 엄지손가락 앞에 빙글빙글도는 보석이 있습니다. 그게

Universe incarnated and carried out his Work of Renewing Heaven and Earth, revealing, "By disassembling and reconstructing heaven and earth, I have firmly and seamlessly woven together *dosu*…" (Dojeon 5:237:1). Only the original master of heaven and earth is capable of reconstructing heaven and earth anew. Father Sangjenim is the Great Healer King who heals all diseases afflicting heaven and earth.

The first event of *gaebyeok* will be a disaster of disease that will sweep across the world. The Healer Dosu is therefore a central theme for this planet. Because disasters of disease—both major and minor—will strike like a typhoon, we must first carry out the Healer Dosu for our own individual survival. Subsequently, the Dosu of the Center for the Healing and Saving of All Nations will be activated to save the world's people, including our families and neighbors.

We will be reborn as immortals during the process of fulfilling the Healer Dosu and the Dosu of the Center for the Healing and Saving of All Nations. Sangjenim attached the Immortal Dosu and the Rejuvenation Dosu to the Healer Dosu. This meant opening a path to overcoming the fundamental obstacle of human history: the fate of birth, aging, sickness, and death. In doing so, he opened a path for people to recover their youthful forms once more.

However, this is not something that can be achieved easily. It requires decades of proper dao cultivation. You must take care of your health, be determined, and perform meditation well.

Upon entering the second stage of meditation, you

마름모 꼴로 왼쪽으로 돌아가는 데요, 이것을 예식을 통해 내려 받으면 이제 시간을 되돌려 갱소년을 시키면서 신선의 몸으로 전환되게 됩니다. 정말로 놀라운 수행을 2차 수행 때 하게 됩니다.

will begin a meditation process that allows your body to restore its youthful form by halting aging at the cellular level. Generally speaking, time moves from the present into the future. However, the Holy Spirit of Great Radiance, who presides over time, has a jewel that spins in front of his thumb as he sits on his throne. It looks like a diamond and spins counterclockwise. When this is bestowed during a ritual, time reverses and you are rejuvenated, gaining the body of an immortal. The most amazing meditation experience occurs during the second stage of meditation.

"I sent Confucius,
Shakyamuni,
and Jesus to the world,
to serve in my work."
(Sangjenim, Dojeon 2:40)

선려화 문화 전수

Learning
Seollyeohwa Culture

빛의 인간으로 거듭나야

　앞으로 동방신선학교에서 하게 될 삼신조화 수행법의 핵심은, 우리 몸의 하단과 중단과 상단에 빛을 채우는 것입니다. 이를 위해 우리가 시천주주와 태을주를 전수 받고, 1차 수행에 들어가게 됩니다. 그리고 2차 수행을 통해 150세 수명줄을 내려받아야 능히 병란을 넘어 후천세상의 신선의 삶, 빛의 인간의 삶을 살 수 있습니다.

　사람은 나이가 들면 늙어가면서 병들고 모든 게 무너지면서 허망하게 죽습니다. 그런데 사람의 생사는 호흡하는 숨결에 달렸습니다. 우리가 호흡한다는 것은 우주와 일체 된 생명으로 살아있다는 가장 근본되는 증거가 아닙니까? 이 숨결이 끝나는 순간 죽음으로 들어가게 됩니다.

　그럼 인간의 숨결의 근본은 어디에 있을까요? 바로, 가슴에 있는 명줄命줄입니다. 가슴 중앙에 있는 명단에 선천 명줄이 깃들어 있습니다. 쇠줄처럼 단단하지만 이것이 조금씩 풀어지면서 하늘에서 받은 명命을 채우면 죽게 되는 것입니다.

84

Become Reborn as a Being of Light

The core element of Samsin meditation, which we will practice at the Eastern School of Immortality Meditation in the days to come, involves filling the lower *danjeon*, middle *danjeon*, and upper *danjeon* of your body with light. To this end, you will learn the Sicheonjuju and Taeeulju mantras and begin the first stage of meditation. And then, you must attain a 150-year life span through the second stage of meditation in order to overcome the disaster of disease and live the life of an immortal and a human of light in the world of Later Heaven.

People typically get sick as they age. They die in vain, and everything falls apart. Yet, a person's survival depends upon the breath they take. Isn't the fact that we breathe the most fundamental evidence that we live a life of oneness with the universe? As soon as such breathing stops, we enter the stage of death.

So, what is the foundation upon which breathing is based? It is none other than the thread of longevity existing within your chest. The Early Heaven's thread of longevity exists within the middle *danjeon* located in the center of your breast. Though it is originally as strong and tight as steel cable, your thread of longevity unravels little by little, and death occurs when your heaven-set time expires.

When someone suffering depression says they want to die, their thread of longevity trembles. Their thread of

우울증이 걸려서 내가 죽고 싶다는 소리를 하면 명줄이 흔들립니다. 명줄이 새들새들 흔들립니다. 그러니까 '나는 꼭 강건하게 바르게 살겠다. 가족과 더불어 조화롭게 살겠다'는 다짐을 해야 우울증도 사라지게 된다.

호흡수행을 바탕으로 자신의 몸에 우주의 근본 빛을 채워넣어야 됩니다. 그래야 자꾸 밝아지고 어둠을 극복할 수 있는 것입니다.

longevity flutters. So, your depression will also go away when you make a pledge to be strong and upright and to live in harmony with your family.

People must fill their bodies with the fundamental light of the cosmos through breathing meditation. By doing so, they can continually become brighter and overcome darkness.

왜 시천주주와 태을주를 수행해야 하는가?

그럼 왜 우리가 삼신조화 수행을 하면서 시천주주侍天主呪와 태을주太乙呪를 읽어야 될까요?

우주와 인간 몸에는 동일하게 다섯가지 영성요소인 정신혼백의精神魂魄意가 있습니다. 그런데 우주의 정신精神은 주재 삼신이신 상제上帝님이 주관하시고, 우주의 혼백魂魄은 자연 삼신이신 무극 삼신 조화 성령聖靈님이 주장하십니다.

대자연의 근본에 계신 삼신일체상제님과 본체삼신이신 태허령님 두 분이 일체가 돼서 우주의 무궁한 그 조화 도道 세계를 구성하고 있습니다. 한마디로, 우주의 정신이 체라면, 우주의 혼백은 용입니다. 우주 율려律呂 세계입니다.

결론적으로 말해서 우주의 정신精神을 받아들이는 것은 시천주주이고, 우주의 혼백魂魄을 받아들이는 것이 태을주입니다.

그래서 진정한 수행자라면 시천주주와 태을주를 조화되게 늘 감사한 마음으로 균형되게 읽는 것이 가장

WHY MUST WE MEDITATE CHANTING THE SICHEONJUJU AND TAEEULJU MANTRAS?

Why is it that the Sicheonjuju and Taeeulju mantras must be chanted when performing Samsin meditation?

Both the universe and the human body possess five spiritual elements: essence, spirit, heavenly soul, earthly soul, and will. The essence and spirit of the cosmos are governed by Sangjenim, while the heavenly soul and earthly soul of the cosmos are governed by the Primal Samsin.

Sangjenim and the Holy Spirit of Great Emptiness (the principal of the Primal Samsin)—who are separate entities—become one and, in doing so, make up the infinite realm of the creation-transformation of the universe. Put simply, if the essence and spirit of the cosmos are the substance, the heavenly soul and earthly soul of the cosmos are the function. Together they make up the cosmic *yullyeo* realm.

To get to the heart of the matter, the Sicheonjuju Mantra is for receiving the essence and spirit of the universe, while the Taeeulju Mantra is for receiving the heavenly soul and earthly soul of the universe.

So, for a true meditator, the most important thing is always chanting these two mantras—the Sicheonjuju and Taeeulju mantras—in balance and with gratitude so that there is harmony between them. This is the practice for

중요합니다. 그게 내 몸에 우주 정신혼백을 채우는 공부입니다.

시천주주와 태을주 공부가 이번 병란 개벽에 내가 진정으로 살고 모든 걸 극복하는 길이며, 통通공부를 가장 빨리 여는 조화 도통공부의 밑천이 되는 것입니다.

그리고 우주율려의 조화 빛꽃인 선려화를 전수 받아서 우주의 정신혼백을 채우게 됩니다. 우주 본체의 절대조화의 근원과 합체되는 놀라운 수행법입니다. 1차 수행의 결론으로 선려화를 내려받고, 이를 바탕으로 2차 수행에서 후천 수명줄을 내려받게 됩니다.

filling your body with the essence, spirit, heavenly soul, and earthly soul of the cosmos.

Sicheonjuju Mantra and Taeeulju Mantra meditation is the path to living a genuine life and surviving the disaster of disease during the coming time of *gaebyeok*. It is the basis of all meditation, and it offers the quickest path to attaining enlightenment.

You will also be able to fill your body with the essence, spirit, heavenly soul, and earthly soul of the cosmos by receiving the Seollyeohwa—the flower of light, the flower of cosmic *yullyeo*. This is an amazing form of meditation that allows you to unite with the source of ultimate creation-transformation stemming from the substance of the universe. The ultimate purpose of the first stage of meditation is receiving the Seollyeohwa. This is the basis upon which your Later Heaven life span is received during the second stage of meditation.

신선 몸을 만드는
1차 수행의 여덟가지 항목

이제 1차 수행의 핵심을 여덟가지 항목을 둘씩 묶어서 크게 4가지로 살펴볼까 합니다.

첫째, 삼신상제님의 조화빛실 받기와 광선여의봉 만들기입니다.

우주의 조물주이신 삼신일체 상제上帝님과 태허령太虛靈님의 법신의 손을 잡아 조화광채를 손에 감는 예식을 올리게 됩니다. 이를 통해 손에 감아 놓은 조화광채를 풀어서 광선여의봉을 만들어서 몸의 근원적인 정화를 할 수 있습니다. 우리 몸의 중심의 충맥과 임독맥을 뚫고 아픈 곳을 치유할 수 있게 됩니다.

둘째, 삼신 조화신선 수행의 동반자인 광선아기 낳기와 언청계용신 만나기입니다.

수행자가 신선으로 성숙하는 과정을 이끌어주는 구도의 동반자인 광선아기(광선씨)와 몸의 수화가 조화롭게 되어 태어나는 망량신이자 수호법신인 '언청계용신'을 만나게 되는 놀라운 수행입니다.

THE EIGHT STEPS OF THE FIRST STAGE OF MEDITATION FOR AN IMMORTAL BODY

Now, let us examine the eight steps of the first stage of meditation in pairs, making four broader categories.

The first pair of steps are: receiving Samsin Sangjenim's thread of creation-transformation light; creating a wish-fulfilling rod of light.

Here you will perform a ritual to hold hands with the dharma bodies of Sangjenim and the Holy Spirit of Great Emptiness. In doing so, you will wrap their light around your wrists. Then, you will unfurl their light and use it to create a rod of light to fundamentally purify your body. You will then be able to unclog your penetrating, governing, and conception vessels to heal the sick areas of your body.

The second pair of steps are: first, giving birth to a baby of light to serve as a companion on your journey of Samsin creation-transformation immortality meditation; second, encountering your personal *eoncheong-gyeyongsin* spirit.

This is an amazing process of meditation in which the meditator meets: their baby of light, who will be the meditator's companion who facilitates maturation into an immortal; and their *eoncheong-gyeyongsin* spirit, who is formed by the water and fire energies in the meditator's body and who is the meditator's guardian spirit and *mangnyang* spirit.

셋째, 삼신 조화신주 백광여의주 만들기와 삼신망량님의 도통심법 전수받기입니다.

상제님과 태허령님의 법신의 기운을 이마 중심에 모시고 삼신조화 여의주인 신주神珠를 만드는 수행을 하고, 본체 삼신님들이 주재하시는 마음과 시간과 공간 세계를 아는 도통 비밀 지도를 전수받아 우주와 하나되는 도통 심법을 전수 받고, 전생의 트라우마를 치유하게 됩니다.

일심을 얻으려면 깊은 밤에 상단에 모셔놓은 신주에 들어가서 수행하시면 됩니다. 그러면 일순간에 우주의 주재자 상제님과 본체삼신이신 우주의 조물주 태허령님과 같은 마음을 얻게 됩니다. 실제로 체험해 보셔야 합니다. 백광 여의주에서 백광이 나와서 이마 밖으로 물결치면서 백광이 너울너울 흘러나가는 것을 보면 정말 멋집니다. 우리 구도자가 상제님과 태허령님을 상단에 모시고 산다는 것이 얼마나 영광입니까. 신주를 모신다는 것은 진선미眞善美의 극치를 뜻합니다.

넷째, 빛의 몸(뼈, 장기)를 만들고, 우주율려 조화빛꽃인 선려화 전수받기입니다.

천지의 어머니 하나님이신 태모님으로부터 빛의 뼈를 만드는 은혜를 전수받게 됩니다. 그리고 삼신조화 칠성령님으로부터 빛의 장부를 만드는 은총을 받게 되

The third pair of steps are: first, creating the Divine Pearl of Samsin Creation-Transformation—the wish-fulfilling pearl of white light; second, learning Samsin Mangnyang's fundamental mindset of enlightenment.

These two steps involve: first, receiving energy from the dharma bodies of Sangjenim and the Holy Spirit of Great Emptiness inside the center of your forehead and meditating to form the Divine Pearl, the wish-fulfilling pearl of Samsin; second, receiving the secret map of enlightenment to understand the Primal Samsin's realms of mind, time, and space in order to attain the mindset of being one with the universe; and, third, healing all trauma from your past lives.

If you want to attain the state of one mind, deep at night enter the Divine Pearl enshrined in your upper *danjeon* and there meditate. In doing so, you will instantly gain the same mind as: Sangjenim, the Ruler of the Universe; the Holy Spirit of Great Emptiness, who is the Cosmic Creator and the principal Primal Samsin. You really must experience this for yourself. It is truly an amazing sight to see the white light beaming from the luminous white wish-fulfilling pearl in the middle of your forehead. It is a true honor for us seekers to live enshrining Sangjenim and the Holy Spirit of Great Emptiness in our upper *danjeon*s. Enshrining the Divine Pearl within oneself signifies the pinnacle of truth, goodness, and beauty.

The fourth pair of steps are: first, making your body into a body of light (including your bones and organs); second, receiving the Seollyeohwa—the flower of light, the flower of cosmic *yullyeo*.

게 됩니다. 그리고 이를 바탕으로 마고 삼신할머니와 궁희, 소희 마마로부터 율려조화 신권을 받아 신선몸을 만들어 가는 선려화를 전수받게 됩니다.

By carrying out these steps, you will fill your bones with light from Taemonim, God the Mother of heaven and earth. You will also receive light from the Seven Holy Spirits to fill your organs. And based on this, you will receive a Seollyeohwa, the flower of *yullyeo* creation-transformation, from Grandmother Mago and Sacred Mothers Gunghui and Sohui. And with this Seollyeohwa, you will be able to transform your body into an immortal body.

선려화 전수 예식

이제 선려화를 내려받는 예식에 들어가는데요. 그 전에 예식을 이해할 수 있도록 간략히 정리해 드리려고 합니다.

사회자가 예식을 선언하면, 천상의 율려천에 있는 마고 삼신 태원성모님이 '때가 됐다. 내려가자' 해서 한순간에 이곳으로 내려오십니다. 마고할머니가 실제로 내려오셔서 꽃을 내려주시는 것입니다. 그리고 마고 삼신할머니와 두 따님인 궁희·소희 마마님이 각각 흰꽃과 붉은꽃과 파란꽃을 내려줍니다. 이것을 합쳐서 무지개빛꽃을 만들게 됩니다.

먼저 마고할머니께 '이제 백색꽃을 내려주십니다' 하면 백색꽃이 조화로 쫙 내려오십니다. 이것은 조화造化 법입니다. 가상현실이 아닙니다. 백색의 꽃이 내려와 구도자의 머리에 쫙쫙쫙쫙 꽂히게 됩니다. 그런데 만약 영안이 어두운 분은 그냥 '나에게도 백색꽃이 지금 내려와서 머리로 딱 들어오고 있다'고 생각하십시오. 눈에 보이는 사람처럼 이미지화를 잘해야 실감 나게 잘 들어옵니다.

THE RITUAL OF RECEIVING THE SEOLLYEOHWA

Now, we will begin the ritual for receiving the Seollyeo-hwa. Before that, I would like to briefly summarize the ritual to aid your understanding of the procedure.

When the host announces the beginning of the ritual, Grandmother Mago, residing in Yullyeocheon Heaven, will instantly descend to this place. Grandmother Mago actually descends and bestows a flower upon you. Grandmother Mago and her daughters, Sacred Mothers Gunghui and Sohui, each bless you with a flower of a different color: white, red, and blue. These flowers are combined to create the rainbow-colored flower of light.

First, when you say to Grandmother Mago, "Now please bestow upon me the flower of white light," the white flower will descend upon you with the power of creation-transformation. This all occurs based on the principle of creation-transformation. The white flower descends and is planted in the seeker's head. But if your spiritual eye has not yet opened, just think, "A white flower is coming down to me right now and being planted directly into my head." To make this feel real, you have to visualize it as though you were actually seeing it.

몸에다가 흰색꽃을 심고 주문을 읽으면 어떻게 될까요? 몸에서 꽃이 분화가 되면서 작은 꽃들이 수백, 수천, 수만, 수억 송이가 세포 단위까지 쫙 밀고 들어갑니다. 그걸 봐야 됩니다. 영안으로 선려화가 분화되는 것을 보는 첫 경험이 중요합니다. 영원히 잊지 못하는 놀라운 체험을 처음에 해야 합니다.

그러려면 잡념을 끊어야 됩니다. 일체 잡념을 끊고 집중해야 합니다. 생각을 내면을 향해서 돌려야 하고, 원십자의 중앙 점 하나를 생각해야 합니다. 그만큼 초집중을 해야 합니다. 나를 잃어버리고 혼몽의 경계에서 도가 열리는 겁니다.

잡념을 갖거나 불신을 하고 사물과 내가 구분되면 의식이 찢어져 있기 때문에 실제 진리의 참모습을 전혀 볼 수가 없습니다. 의식을 내면으로 돌리고 나를 잃어버리고 집중하시기 바랍니다.

분화가 끝나면 흰색꽃을 생각으로 쭉 훑어서 머리 위로 다시 빼내야 합니다. 그리고 두 번째 단계로 궁희, 소희 마마님께서 붉은꽃과 파란꽃을 내려주십니다. 백회 위로 다시 뽑아 올린 흰꽃의 중심에 꽂아주십니다. 꽃 지름은 13센티, 길이는 15센티 정도 됩니다. 머리통만 한 제법 큰 꽃이죠. 그러면 세 개의 꽃이 몸에 심고 수억 송이로 분화를 시키십시오. 그리고 나서 다시 쭉

What happens when you chant a mantra after this white flower is planted in your body? As the flower divides within you, hundreds, thousands, and even millions of small flowers spread out and enter your cells. This is something you really must see. Your first experience seeing the division of the Seollyeohwa with your spiritual eye is very important. You really must have this amazing experience for yourself. It is something that you will never forget.

To have this experience, you must cease all random thoughts. You must stop all random thoughts and concentrate. You have to turn your consciousness inward and focus with one mind. That is how focused you have to be. You will lose your ego, and dao will open to you in the realm of obscurity.

If you have random thoughts or if you distrust the process and isolate yourself from your connection to all things, your consciousness will be divided, completely preventing you from seeing truth in its genuine form. Please turn your consciousness inward, leave your ego behind, and concentrate.

When the process of division is complete, you must use your thoughts to gather the white flowers and bring them back up to the top of your head. After that, the second step will occur: Sacred Mothers Gunghui and Sohui will bestow the red and blue flowers upon you. They place them in the center of the white flower that was brought back above the crown chakra. Each flower is thirteen centimeters in diameter and fifteen centimeters tall. They're quite big flowers that are about the size of your head. Next, you plant these three types of flowers in

훑어서 한 송이로 만듭니다.

　그리고 마지막 단계로 마고 삼신할머니께 기도올리면 순식간에 일곱 가지 무지개색의 빛꽃으로 바뀌게 됩니다. 그러면 선려화가 완성된 것입니다. 완성이 된 선려화는 상단에 모시면 됩니다.

　이제 예식을 하시고, 그 후에 분합하는 수행 실습을 같이 해보겠습니다.

〈 선려화 전수 예식 진행 〉

　다들 수고 많으셨습니다. '우주율려 조화꽃인 선려화를 내려 받는 예식'을 잘 마무리하셨어요. 그런데 누구는 이렇게 속으로 이야기 할 거예요. '아니 이거 믿을 수 있는 건가?', 또 어떤 이는 반대로 '아, 이것은 역사의 기적이다, 우리가 이것을 만나기 위해서 천상과 지상을 오가면서 헤맸구나' 하고 말하기도 합니다.

your body and divide them into hundreds of millions of little flowers. Then you gather them up again and bring them together into a single bouquet.

Now, for the final step, if you pray to Grandmother Mago, this bouquet quickly turns into a flower of white light with seven hues. With that, the Seollyeohwa is complete. All you then have to do is enshrine the completed Seollyeohwa in your upper *danjeon*.

Now, let's perform the ceremony, and then afterwards we'll practice meditation for dividing and fusing the flowers.

[The ritual of receiving Seollyeohwa proceeds.]

Well done, everyone. You have completed the ritual for receiving the Seollyeohwa, the cosmic *yullyeo* flower of creation-transformation. But some of you are likely saying to yourselves, "Can I really believe this?" Others, meanwhile, will say the opposite: "Oh, this is a miracle of history. I've been wandering between heaven and earth to encounter such an experience."

선려화 전수 예식 영상
The ritual of receiving Seollyeohwa

마고 삼신할머니가 선려화를 내려주신 일화

여러분, 도통道通이란 무엇일까요? 수많은 구도자들이 갈구했던 도통이란 무엇이냔 말입니다. 한마디로 도통은 내 몸과 마음에 우주의 율려 조화의 빛을 가득 채우는 것입니다. 끊임없는 수행을 통해 빛으로 내 몸과 마음을 가득 채워 사물의 깊은 이치를 깨닫는 것입니다.

우주의 율려조화를 옴과 훔 소리만 갖고 받을 수 없기 때문에 마고 삼신할머니께서 선려화仙呂花를 내려주신 것입니다. 이에 관한 재미난 일화가 있는데 잠시 전해볼까 합니다.

5천 년 전에 도를 잘 닦아서 신선이 거의 다 된 경계에 있는 젊은 구도자들이 있었습니다. 그들한테 마고 할머니가 등장하셔서 '너는 무엇을 깨달았느냐?' 하고 하문하셨습니다.

첫 번째 청년은 '저는 허허虛虛로운 가운데 빛이 근본인 걸 깨달았습니다', 두 번째 청년은 '무변광대한 우주 가운데서 마음 하나가 제일인 걸 깨달았습니다.'라고 답했습니다. 그리고 세 번째 청년은 '저는 흰 할머니를 본 것이 제 공부의 아주 최상입니다.'라고 답했습니다.

그랬더니 마고 할머니는 세 번째 청년이 당신을 알아보

The Tale of Grandmother Mago Bestowing the Seollyeohwa

Just what is enlightenment? What is this enlightenment that so many seekers have longed for? Put simply, enlightenment is successfully filling your body and mind with the light of cosmic *yullyeo* creation-transformation. It is realizing the sublime principle of all things upon filling your body and mind with this light through unrelenting meditation.

Grandmother Mago bestows the Seollyeohwa because it is impossible to fully receive cosmic *yullyeo* creation-transformation through meditation using the sounds of *om* and *hoom* alone. There is an interesting story about this that I would like to tell you.

Five thousand years ago, there were some young seekers who had nearly reached the point of becoming immortals through devoted dao cultivation. Grandmother Mago appeared before them and asked, "What have you come to realize?"

The first youth answered, "I have come to realize that light is the basis of the center of the emptiest void." The second youth said, "I have come to realize that in the infinite and vast universe, the mind is the most paramount." Lastly, the third youth answered, "Meeting you, O Grandmother White, has been the best part of my cultivation."

Grandmother Mago thus knew that the third youth

니까 '아 이 녀석이 나를 알아보는구나. 기특하구나' 하면서 백색 꽃을 하나 빼서 머리에다 꽂아주셨습니다. 그리고, '이것을 온몸에다 심어라. 그러면 온몸이 다 꽃이 될 것이다'라고 하셨습니다. 그리고서 재차 시험하시면서 물으신 거죠. '너는 심고나면 어떻게 할 것이냐?' 하니 그 청년이 '제가 심었으니 제가 모아야죠'라며 분합의 원리를 말한 겁니다. 그렇게 해서 선려화의 역사가 시작되었습니다.

그런데 한 여자 구도자가 있었습니다. 네 번째 아가씨인데 자기에게는 마고 할머니가 말도 안 붙여주시고 가버리셔서 밤낮 뭐라고 쏭알(투덜)거렸다고 합니다. 그래서 마고 삼신할머니가 '저 녀석 때문에 시끄러워서 못 살겠다. 너희들이 가서 해결하고 와라' 해서 두 딸인 궁희, 소희 마마를 내려가게 합니다.

그래서 두 따님이 파란색과 붉은색 꽃을 내려주게 됩니다. 참 신비롭고도 놀라운 이야기 인데요, 이제 마고 삼신할머니가 내려주시는 흰꽃과 두 따님이 내려주시는 파란꽃과 붉은꽃을 오늘 내려받게 됩니다.

사실 율려천律呂天(직녀성織女星, 베가성)은 지구에서 25광년을 가야 되는 천상의 별입니다. 그런데 마고 삼신할머니와 두 따님께서 한순간에 옥좌玉座를 타고 직접 내려오셔서 우주율려의 조화꽃을 이 자리에서 다 내려주십니다. 이런 은총이 어디 있겠습니까?

had recognized her and responded, "Ah, this young-ster knows who I am. How commendable, indeed." She then produced a single white flower and affixed it to the youth's head. She added, "Plant this throughout your whole body. Do so, and your entire body will become a flower." Then, meaning to test the youth, she asked, "What do you plan to do after planting this flower?" The youth replied, "Having planted the flower, I must afterward gather the flowers," giving voice to the principle of division and fusion. And this third youth's answer is how the history of the Seollyeohwa began.

However, there was another seeker present I'd like to tell you about. She was the fourth such youth present, and yet Grandmother Mago departed without ever saying a single word to her. This left the fourth youth constantly grumbling. Hearing this, Grandmother Mago said to herself, "I cannot endure the noise from that child any longer." She then sent down her two daughters, Sacred Mothers Gunghui and Sohui, to the girl, saying, "You two better go and deal with her."

This is why the two daughters began bestowing the blue and red flowers. This is a truly mystical and amazing story. And now you will have the opportunity to receive the white flower of Grandmother Mago and the blue and red flowers of her two daughters.

Yullyeo Heaven (or Vega) is actually a star located twenty-five light years from earth. In spite of this fact, Grandmother Mago and her two daughters are able to instantly descend riding their jade thrones and bestow upon us the cosmic *yullyeo* flowers of creation-transformation. Where else can you find such a blessing?

마고성 문화는
신선문명의 모체

　인류의 원형문화의 맥은 2만 5천년 전의 마고성麻姑城에서 출발합니다. 마고성의 삼신할머니가 '내가 삼천년을 설계해서 본체 삼신이신 태허령님을 감동하게 했다. 그래서 모든 인간이 조화 신선을 만들어줄 길이 열렸다'고 하십니다. 그래서 마고 할머니가 바이칼 호수에서 나반을 처음 만나 결혼을 하시고 율국律國이라는 국가가 형성된 것입니다.

　율국은 우주의 조화신선의 율려律呂 조화권을 내려주는 신선문명의 모체가 된다는 뜻입니다. 마고성의 율국에서 신선문화가 시작된 것입니다. 이것을 『환단고기』에서는 최초의 인류로 나반那般과 아만阿曼이라고 기록해 놓은 것입니다. 박제상의 『부도지』도 마고문화를 일부 전하지만 후세의 신화 이야기로 남성없이 여성이 애 낳는 것처럼 이야기가 덧붙여진 면도 있습니다. 사실 신선조화 세계는 보통 역사학에서는 신화처럼 보지만, 조화도통세계에서 내려오는 무궁한 이야기들이 있습니다. 이건 천기누설일 정도로 중요한 이야기입니다.

Mago Castle Culture: The Womb of the Civilization of Immortality

The lineage of the archetypal culture of humanity began in Mago Castle twenty-five thousand years ago. Back then, Grandmother Mago said, "I have mapped out three thousand years of history to get the attention of the Holy Spirit of Great Emptiness, the Primal Samsin. This is how the path will open to make all humans into immortals." As part of her plan, Grandmother Mago went to meet Naban at Lake Baikal for the first time. They went onward to marry and establish the country known as 'Yulguk.'

With this, Yulguk became the womb of the civilization of immortality. It bestowed upon future generations the power of *yullyeo* creation-transformation, which enables immortality. The culture of immortality began in Mago Castle, the capital of the nation of Yulguk. This was recorded in *Hwandan Gogi*, which states that Naban and Aman were the very first humans. Though Bak Jesang's *Budoji* partially details Mago culture, it presents Mago culture as the subject of a myth told by future generations; and in this myth, the first woman is presented as having a baby without a male partner. While the world of immortal creation-transformation does indeed look like mythology to mainstream history academia, there are an infinite number of stories attesting to its veracity that have been passed down from the realm of enlighten-

그리고 이후 원형 문화의 맥은 환국과 배달국, 단군 조선의 상고시대를 지나 북부여와 고구려를 통해 전수된 것입니다. 대한의 국통맥을 따라 신선문화의 맥, 선맥仙脈이 전수되었습니다. 삼랑三郎문화가 있었습니다.

ment. These stories are profoundly important revelations from heaven.

The lineage of this archetypal culture was passed down from the period of high antiquity ruled first by Hwanguk, Baedal, and then Dangun Joseon, and then through the reigns of Bukbuyeo and Goguryeo. The lineage of the culture of immortality—the lineage of immortality—has been passed down through the states ruled by the Korean people.

1차 수행의 결론으로 전수 받는
조화빛꽃 선려화

오늘 여러분은 빛꽃, 선려화를 받았습니다. 1차 수행의 결론이 우주의 율려 조화 빛꽃을 받는 과정입니다. 우리가 마고 삼신할머니와 궁희, 소희 마마님으로부터 선려화를 내려받아 대우주의 진정한 최상의 도통 세계에 들어갈 수가 있는 것입니다.

이제 선려화를 몸에 심고 분합分合을 잘해야 합니다. 분화를 위해서는 이마에 모셔놓은 본체 선려화를 복사해서 온몸에 심고 '이제 선려화를 분화합니다' 하면 분화가 시작됩니다.

모든 건 생각과 이미지로 하는 겁니다. 조화 신선 도통 공부는 잡념을 떼고 집중하면 됩니다. 생각대로 되는 문화입니다. 생각이 그대로 되는 겁니다.

머리의 본체 선려화를 복사해서 간에도 심고, 심장에도 심고, 오장육부에 심기 바랍니다. 만약 잇몸이 아프다고 하면 그곳에 심어도 됩니다. 크게 복사해서 붙이거나, 작게 만들어서 장부의 크기에 맞게 심으면 됩니다. 우리의 생각대로 크게 작게 만들어서 심고 분화시

THE SEOLLYEOHWA: THE FLOWER OF LIGHT AND THE CULMINATION OF THE FIRST STAGE OF MEDITATION

Today, you all received a Seollyeohwa, a flower of light. The first stage of meditation culminates in the receiving of this cosmic *yullyeo* flower of creation-transformation. We can enter the true and ultimate world of cosmic enlightenment by receiving the Seollyeohwa from Grandmother Mago and from Sacred Mothers Gunghui and Sohui.

Now you must plant the Seollyeohwa in your body, then thoroughly carry out the process of division and fusion. The process of flower division starts with you making copies of the original Seollyeohwa enshrined in your forehead and planting them throughout your body while announcing, "And so begins the flower division."

Everything in this process is accomplished by thoughts and images. You just have to dispense with random thoughts and focus when carrying out meditation for creation-transformation immortality enlightenment. In this practice, things proceed in the way you imagine. They occur exactly as you think they will.

Please make copies of the original Seollyeohwa in your head and plant them in your liver, heart, and other internal organs. If, for instance, your gums are hurting, plant some there too. You can make copies as big as you desire or make them small enough to match the size of your or-

켰다가 다시 합일하면 됩니다.

그런데 선려화를 몸에 심을 때 주의할 점이 있습니다. 선려화를 몸에 심기 전에 몸을 빛 몸으로 만드는 것을 선행하라는 겁니다. 그래야 선려화의 빛이 들어가서 분합이 잘 됩니다.

한마디로 몸에 빛을 먼저 채워야 합니다. 왜냐하면, 마치 도배를 할 때 풀칠을 하고 벽지를 바르듯이 먼저 빛으로 채우고 그 위에 선려화를 심어야 효과가 좋아집니다.

그래서 만약 여러분이 머리가 아프거나, 치아가 풍치로 인해 쑤시고 아프다면, 우선 예식에 따라 빛으로 환부를 채우고 선려화를 심어보십시오. 5~10분 정도 일심으로 심고, 분합하는 공정을 잘하고 주문을 읽으며 깊게 잠들면 놀랍게도 다음날 그냥 낫게 됩니다.

gans. Your thoughts guide the process as you create flowers of varying sizes, plant them throughout your body, divide them, and fuse them together again.

However, there is something you should first do before planting these Seollyeohwa flowers. You must turn your body into a body of light prior to planting the Seollyeohwa flowers in it. That way, the light of the Seollyeohwas will enter your body and the process of division and fusion will occur properly.

Put simply, you must first fill your body with light. This is the same principle as applying adhesive before installing wallpaper: you have to fill your body with light first and then plant the Seollyeohwa flowers to improve the effect.

So, for example, if you have a headache or your teeth are aching from gum disease, you should first fill the affected area with light and then plant the Seollyeohwa flowers as was done in the ritual. If you spend five to ten minutes properly carrying out the process of planting, dividing, and fusing these flowers while chanting the mantras with one mind and then entering a deep sleep, you will feel amazingly good.

선려화를 심고 합일하며
온몸이 선려화 자체가 돼야

그리고 선려화를 심을 때는 힘차게 심어야 합니다. 오장육부에 힘차게 심고 분화와 합일을 해야 합니다. 나아가 세포 하나하나 속의 미토콘드리아까지 양자 단위까지 들어가야 합니다.

그럼 왜 그렇게 해야 하는 걸까요? 우리가 궁극의 마음을 체험하기 위해서입니다. 태허령의 무無의 세계, 무극無極의 조화망량세계를 알아야 우리의 마음 세계를 체험하게 됩니다. 태허령님의 무극세계는 빛밖에 없습니다. 아무런 일체 형상이란 게 없는 조화세계입니다. 우리가 삼신조화 수행을 통해 몸을 빛체로 만들면서 조화세계로 들어가야 합니다.

시천주주를 송주하면서 선려화를 심어봅시다. 잡념을 갖고 하면 50% 안쪽으로 효율이 떨어지니 집중集中과 몰입沒入을 해서 90%, 100%의 효율로 높여야 합니다. 그래야 빛을 채울 수 있고, 치유도 잘 됩니다.

선려화 분화는 장기에 심는 것이고, 합체는 내 몸 자체가 선려화가 되는 것입니다. 조화로운 빛으로 내 몸

PLANT AND FUSE THE SEOLLYEOHWA; BECOME A SEOLLYEOHWA

You must plant the Seollyeohwa flowers with vigor. Vigorously plant them in your five viscera and six entrails, divide them further, then fuse them together again. You must plant them even as deep as the mitochondria of each cell—even as deep as the subatomic realm of your cells.

This is so that you can directly experience the ultimate mind. You must understand the Holy Spirit of Great Emptiness's realm of nothingness—the *mangnyang* realm of the creation-transformation of Mugeuk—in order to experience the realm of your mind. In the Holy Spirit of Great Emptiness's realm of nothingness, there is nothing but light. This is a completely formless realm of creation-transformation. You must enter the realm of creation-transformation as you turn your body into a body of light through Samsin meditation.

Let's try planting the Seollyeohwa flowers while chanting the Sicheonjuju Mantra. If you possess random thoughts, your efficiency will decline by as much as fifty percent. This means you must focus and immerse yourself in your practice to increase your efficiency to ninety percent, or even to one hundred percent. That way, you can fill yourself with light, and healing will occur effectively.

The division of the Seollyeohwa is done so the flower

을 채운다는 생각으로 3~5분을 기준으로 분화와 합일을 해야 합니다. 몸이 안 좋은 곳은 20~30분 집중해서 분화와 합체를 하면 통증이 다 가실 정도가 될 것입니다.

만약 여러분 중에 코에 축농증이 있다면 코 위에도 하나 심고, 옆에도 심어서 분합을 해 보십시오.

힘차게 심고, 시천주주 도공을 따라서 춤을 추듯이 자연스럽게 움직이면서 세포 깊은 곳까지 심고, 분화를 시키기 바랍니다.

분화를 잘해야 합니다. 분화는 내 몸에 선려화를 완벽하게 꽂는 것이고, 합일은 내 몸 자체가 빛꽃이 되는 것을 말합니다. 즉, 몸 세포와 하나되게 심고, 분화해서 합일시켜야 합니다.

경추를 비롯해 각 척추에 선려화를 심고 분합을 해 보십시오. '나는 경추가 안 좋다. 척추 디스크가 있다'는 분은 대개 생활 속에서 자세가 바르지 못해서 오는 병인데요, 이런 분들은 품격있게 바르게 앉으려고 노력해야 합니다. 몸이 안 좋으면 베개를 베고 누워서도 선려화 수행을 할 수 있습니다.

선려화 분합수행은 얼마든지 자유롭게 할 수 있습니다. 또한, 요즘은 뼈와 장부와 신경과 관련된 좋은 자료가 많습니다. 이를 보면서 곳곳에 섬세하게 선려화

can be planted in your various organs. Fusing the copied flowers again ends with turning your body itself into a Seollyeohwa. You must spend at least three to five minutes dividing and fusing the Seollyeohwa while thinking about filling your body with harmonious light. If you spent twenty to thirty minutes dividing, planting, and fusing the Seollyeohwa while focusing on places where your body is ill, the pain will go away.

If any of you have a sinus infection, try dividing the flower, planting one on the top of your nose and one on the side of your nose, and then fusing the flowers together again.

Please plant the flowers vigorously and move around as if dancing while performing dynamic Sicheonjuju Mantra meditation. While doing so, plant the divided flowers deep within your cells and divide them further.

Flower division must be done with care. This process of division involves planting the Seollyeohwas throughout your entire body. The process of fusion involves affixing countless Seollyeohwa flowers to your body, turning your body itself into a flower of light. In other words, plant them in your cells, then divide them further and ultimately fuse them with the cells in your body.

Plant Seollyeohwas in each vertebrae disk, then carry out the process of division and fusion. "My cervical vertebrae are in poor condition. I have a vertebra disk issue." Those to whom this statement applies should try to sit upright with dignity, as this is a condition that usually comes from poor posture in your daily life. If you are not feeling well, you can practice Seollyeohwa meditation even when lying down with a pillow.

를 심고 분합수행을 하시면 더욱 좋습니다. 선려화는 빛 덩어리이기 때문에 세포에 넣을 때 확 찔러 넣는다는 식으로 해도 전혀 부작용이 없습니다. 이것은 우주의 절대 조화 율려의 꽃입니다.

You are free to practice Seollyeohwa division and fusion meditation as you please. There is a lot of good information on bone, organ, and nervous system health these days. It is even better if you can reference anatomical images or charts while performing meditation for planting, dividing, and fusing the Seollyeohwa while focusing on each part of your body. The Seollyeohwa is a bundle of light, so there won't be any side effects when you insert them straight into your cells. This is the sublime creation-transformation *yullyeo* flower of the universe.

66

Seollyeohwa ('Flower of Cosmic Light')
meditation is an amazing form of meditation
that allows you to unite with the source
of ultimate creation-transformation
of the universe.

99

123

K-Spirit
치유문화 세계로

K-Spirit Healing
Culture
Goes Global

지금은 우주의 환절기, 여름철 극단의 때

그동안 인류는 우주 1년, 12만9,600이라는 큰 주기 아래 살아왔습니다.

지금은 인간농사 짓는 우주 1년의 봄여름 선천先天 세상이 끝나고, 이제 가을의 후천後天 세상으로 넘어가는 여름철의 아주 극단의 말기입니다. 지금 전문가들은 기후 변화와 생태계 파괴를 얘기하며 지구 기온이 높아짐을 걱정합니다. 그러나 고온 현상은 이산화탄소만의 문제가 아닙니다. 근본적인 이유는 지금이 불의 계절인 여름철 말기이기 때문입니다.

지금 인류는 우주의 환절기換節期에서 병란病亂을 만났습니다. 여름철 불의 계절이 끝나고 가을철로 들어가는 개벽開闢의 중심 시간대에서 헐떡거리고 있는 것입니다.

단언컨대 우주의 시간법칙인 인간농사 짓는 우주 1년, 12만9,600년의 근본 이치를 모르면 이 세상 어떤 문제도 속시원하게 해결되지 못합니다. 인간농사 짓는 천리天理부터 파악해야 합니다.

Now Is the Transition Point of the Cosmic Seasons, the Peak of Summer

Humanity has always lived in accordance with the great cycle of the cosmic year, which contains 129,600 earth years. In the cosmic year, the Early Heaven's cosmic spring and summer, when humans are cultivated, are now coming to an end as we reach the very last stage of summer's final age—the threshold of passing into the cosmic autumn of the Later Heaven. Experts now talk about climate change and ecosystem destruction and worry about rising global temperatures. But high temperatures are not just a problem arising from carbon dioxide. The fundamental cause is that the world is at the end of the cosmic summer, when the fire energy is most intense.

Today's humanity is experiencing disasters of disease that occur during this transition point of the cosmic seasons. We are struggling through the early stages of *gaebyeok* that will transition us into the cosmic autumn after the cosmic summer's season of fire ends.

None of the problems facing this world can be solved adequately without an understanding of the fundamental principle underlying this law of cosmic time: the cosmic year in which humans are cultivated for 129,600 earth years. Everything must be understood in light of the heavenly principle of humanity's cultivation.

우주 1년 창조 이법:
우주의 선·후천 개벽 운동

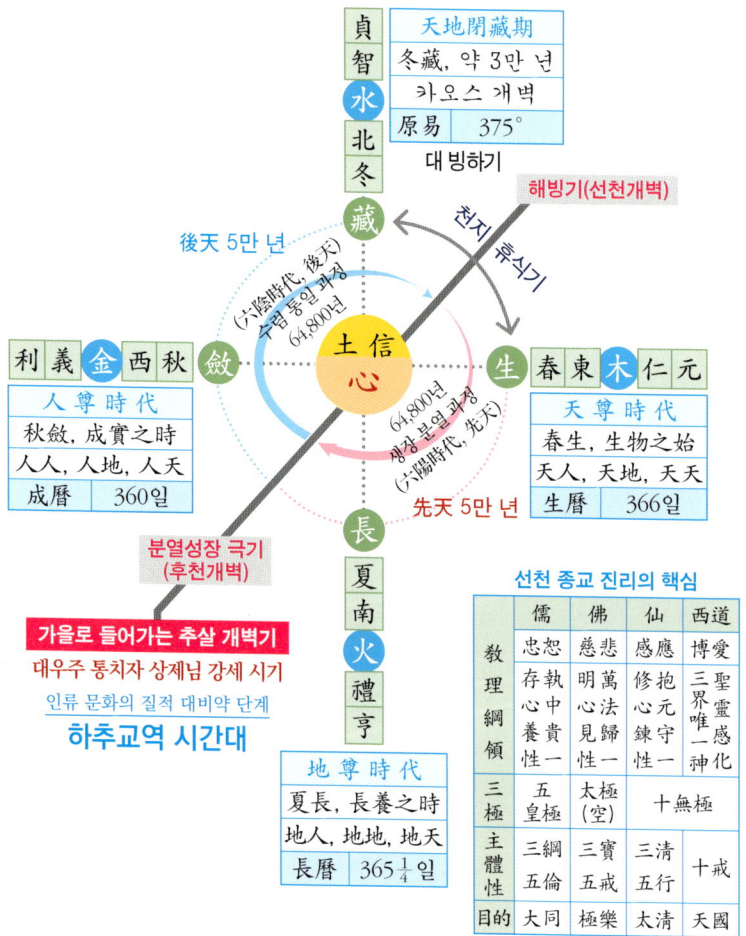

안운산 태상종도사님이 상제님의 지상 강세 소식과 가을개벽 후천선경의 도래, 태을주로 천하창생을 구원하는 이치를 한 장의 도표로 담아 도기 76(1946)년에 처음으로 공표하셨다. 이후 안경전 종도사님이 우주일년의 가르침을 널리 대중화시키셨다.

The Cosmic Year

(129,600 Calendar Years)

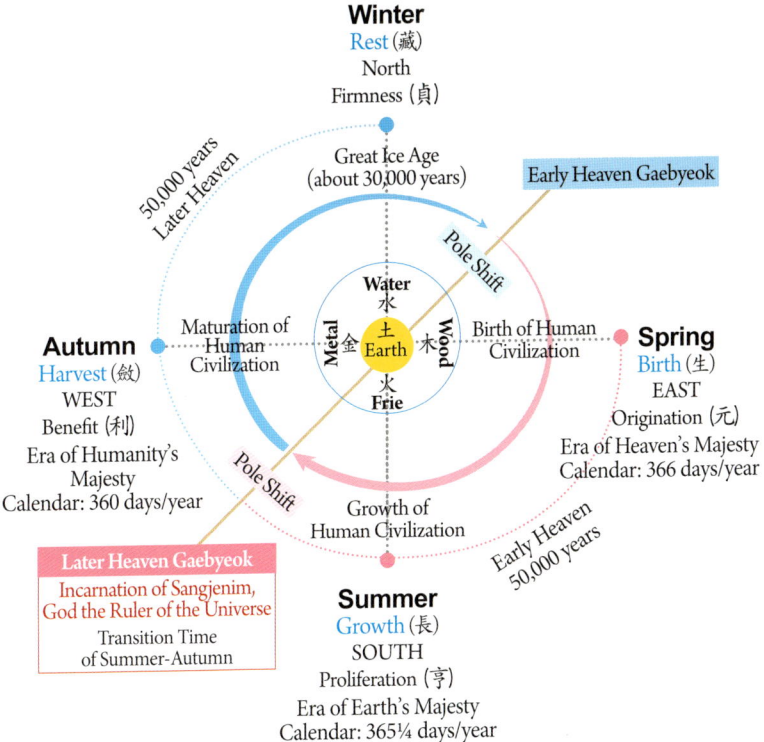

The Civilization of the Later Heaven

· Union of Spirits and Humans
· Civilization of Omniscience
· Civilization of Sublime Dao Mastery Through Enlightenment into the Mind
· Civilization of Enlightenment
· Immortal Paradise of Creation-Transformation

In 1946, Ahn Un-san, the Taesang Jongdosanim of Jeung San Do, first drew the cosmic year diagram to illustrate the greatest changes impacting the human world: the human incarnation of Sangjenim and the imminent arrival of the Later Heaven Gaebyeok. For many decades, Ahn Gyeong-jeon, the Jongdosanim of Jeung San Do, has been spreading this teaching across the world.

빛의 인간으로,
신선 조화인간으로

오늘 동방신선학교 출범을 통해 자연개벽과 문명개벽과 인간개벽의 세벌 개벽을 성취하는 빛꽃의 신선 조화인간을 만들어 나가는 대장정이 본격화되기 시작했습니다.

동방신선학교를 통해 삼신조화 수행법의 정수를 맛보시기 바랍니다.

다시 강조하지만 선려화는 시간만 나면 심고 분합해야 합니다. 갑상선이 안 좋다고 하면 그곳을 생각하고 선려화를 뽑아서 중간 크기로 해서 심으시고, 또 간이 안 좋다 하면 그곳에는 큰 것을 가져다가 심어보시기 바랍니다. 그리고는 분화를 명하시고 주문을 5~10분 정성껏 송주하시고, 다시 합일을 하면 됩니다. 온몸에 꽃을 심고 분합을 하시기 바랍니다.

이게 숙달이 되면 재봉틀 박듯이 꽃을 빠르게 심을 수 있습니다. 그래서 선려화 공부에 재미가 들리면 깊은 밤 5시간도 신나서 수행하면서 '아, 이제 아침이 밝아오는구나' 할 정도가 됩니다. 그러면 온몸에 꽃을 수

BECOMING HUMANS OF LIGHT, IMMORTAL HUMANS OF CREATION-TRANSFORMATION

Starting today with the launch of the Eastern School of Immortality Meditation, the long journey has begun in earnest to develop immortal humans of the flower of light—humans who will bring to fruition the three stages of *gaebyeok*: the *gaebyeok* of nature, the *gaebyeok* of civilization, and the *gaebyeok* of humanity.

We hope you will experience the essence of Samsin meditation through the Eastern School of Immortality Meditation.

I cannot stress this enough: you must carry out the process of Seollyeohwa planting, division, and fusion whenever you have spare time. If you are having thyroid issues, visualize making copies of medium-sized Seollyeohwa and planting them in the afflicted area. If your liver is ailing, take a big flower and plant it there. Then, divide the flower, chant sincerely for five to ten minutes, and fuse the flower together again. Please plant flowers throughout your body and carry out the process of division and fusion.

Once you've mastered this, you can plant flowers as quickly as though using a sewing machine. Having learned to enjoy Seollyeohwa meditation, you will find yourself excitedly meditating even for five hours straight, deep into the night, then suddenly realizing, "Oh, it's al-

만, 백만 송이 심는 겁니다. 빛의 꽃을 심는 겁니다. 선려화 심기에 달관하려면 피아노 치듯, 언어를 배우는 것처럼 노력해야 합니다. 점점 숙달되면 즐겁게 할 수 있습니다.

ready morning." When that happens, you'll have planted tens of thousands, or even millions, of copies of this flower throughout your body. You'll have planted flowers of light. You have to invest a great deal of effort if you want to master planting the Seollyeohwa, similar to striving to learn the piano or a language. You'll increasingly enjoy the process the better you get at it.

생활 수행을 통해
선려화를 심고 합일해야

그리고 병란을 극복하기 위해서는 생활 수행이 중요합니다. 아침에 일어나서 장부에 선려화仙呂花를 심어보십시오. 상단에 있는 원본을 복사해서 큰 꽃을 머리에다가 하나 심고, 가슴과 폐와 간에도 한두 송이 심으시고, 중간 크기의 꽃을 만들어서 소장과 대장 등에 심으면 큰 효과를 보게 됩니다.

꽃을 심을 때는 집중해서, 정확하게 심는 위치를 잡아서 착착 심으시면 됩니다. 그렇게 3~5분 단위로 심고 분화하시고, 합체를 하시면 됩니다. 어려워 마시고 전체 몸에다가 선려화를 심고, 신나게 힘차게 분화와 합체를 하시면 되는 것입니다. 선려화 수행은 짧은 시간, 바쁜 아침시간에도 할 수 있습니다.

누구던 시간 날 때 5~10분 심고 주문을 노래하듯 송주하면 됩니다. 그렇게 하면 빛꽃이 몸을 치유하면서 기분도 좋아집니다. 또 몸이 아픈 분은 직접 통증이 있는 데를 먼저 하시면 됩니다. 우선 환부의 염증을 가라앉혀 통증을 잡고, 전체 몸에다가 심고 분합수행을 하

PLANT AND FUSE THE SEOLLYEOHWA THROUGH DAILY MEDITATION

Now, daily meditation is important in overcoming disasters of disease. Try planting the Seollyeohwa in your organs when you wake up in the morning. Make copies of the original version located in your upper *danjeon* and plant a large one in your head, then one or two in your chest, lungs, and liver. Then make medium-sized flowers and plant them in various locations, such as your small and large intestines. Do so, and you will receive great benefits.

Concentrate when planting these flowers, establish a precise location, and then plant them one after another. Plant, divide, and fuse them in that way in intervals of three to five minutes. There's no need to struggle with it. Plant Seollyeohwas all over your body, then enthusiastically carry out the process of division and fusion. Seol-lyeo-hwa meditation can be carried out for a short amount of time, even in the morning when you are busy.

Anyone with spare time can spend five to ten minutes planting and chanting mantras as if singing. Do that and your mood will improve as the flower of light heals your body. Those who are experiencing pain should first focus this procedure on the centers of pain. First, plant the flowers in specific areas to alleviate pain and inflammation, and then plant them all over your body. Afterwards, proceed with Seollyeohwa division and fusion medita-

시면 됩니다.

선려화 수행을 위해서 우리가 인체의 주요 장부와 근육에 대해서는 어느 정도 알아야 합니다. 왜냐하면, 우리가 몸을 아는 만큼 더 미세하게 아는 만큼 정확하게 빛꽃을 심고 치유할 수 있기 때문입니다. 앞으로 선려화 수행을 통해 소중한 우리 몸을 좀 더 밝고 건강하게 만들어나가시길 바랍니다.

tion.

You must have a certain degree of knowledge about the main organs and muscles of the human body for Seol-lyeohwa meditation. The reason for this is that the more precisely we understand our bodies, the more precision we can bring to planting flowers of light and carrying out healing. In the days to come, please make your precious body a little brighter and healthier using Seollyeohwa meditation.

후천 수명줄을 내려받아야

가을개벽기에 선천 명줄은 다 끊어지게 됩니다. 지금은 후천 수명줄을 내려받아야 합니다. 우리가 후천 수명줄을 받기 위해서는 본체 삼신님의 조화기운을 받아서 명단에 삼태극 명주를 세팅해야 합니다.

우선 오늘 전수해드린 선려화를 심고, 분합을 자주해야 합니다. 몸을 변화시켜면서 후천 수명줄을 내려받을 수 있도록 좀 더 적극적으로 임해주셔야 합니다.

지금 천상의 대신선들은 하루에 몇 시간씩 수행할까요? 도통하신 신선님이 한결같이 말씀하시기를 '하루에 최소 열 시간 이상씩 수행한다'고 하십니다. 마고 할머니도 '나도 열 시간 이상을 한다'고 하십니다. 그러니 우리도 그분들을 본받아서 하루에 최대한 많은 시간을 수행하려 해야 합니다.

사실 가을개벽을 앞두고 하루에 30분, 1시간 한다는 것은 말이 안 되는 이야기입니다. 최대한 몰입을 해서 틈만 있으면 선려화를 심고 분화하시고 합일시켜야 합니다. 시천주주와 태을주 주송 MP3를 따라서 수행하시면 됩니다.

YOU MUST RECEIVE A LATER HEAVEN LIFE SPAN

The Early Heaven's threads of longevity will be completely severed during the Autumn Gaebyeok. You must now receive a Later Heaven life span. In order to receive a Later Heaven life span, you must first receive the creation-transformation energy of the Primal Samsin and place the Samtaegeuk ("Three Taegeuk") Pearl of Longevity in your middle *danjeon*.

First, you must regularly plant and carry out the division and fusion process of the Seollyeohwa that you received today. You must apply yourself even more actively while transforming your body in order to be bestowed a Later Heaven life span.

How many hours do you think the immortals in heaven are currently performing meditation each day? All the enlightened immortals say the same thing: "At a minimum, I meditate for more than ten hours a day." Grandmother Mago always says, "I meditate for more than ten hours a day, too." We must, therefore, emulate these esteemed ones by performing meditation as much as possible in the span of a day.

In truth, with the Autumn Gaebyeok nearing, it doesn't make sense to spend just thirty minutes or an hour a day on meditation. You should be as immersed as you can be, planting, dividing, and fusing Seollyeohwas whenever you have a chance. You can meditate while following along with audio recordings of the Sicheonjuju and Taeeulju mantras.

도통조화 신선문화를 적극적으로 배워야

상제님은 '병란이 거센 태풍처럼 앞으로 몰려온다'고 하셨습니다. 지금은 인간농사 짓는 우주 1년 속 인간 씨종자를 추리는 때입니다. 따라서 병란 개벽기에 사랑하는 가족이 한 사람도 빠짐없이 희생되지 않도록, 후천 수명줄을 받는 삼신조화 수행법을 배워야 합니다.

지구는 우주의 핵核입니다. 우리 인간 한 사람 한 사람이 우주의 소중한 기적입니다. 그래서 누구에게도 잘해줘야 됩니다. 존경해줘야 합니다. 만약 상처를 주고 잘못한 것이 있으면 용서를 구해야 합니다. 그리고 이제 인류사에 삼신조화 수행법을 통해 모든 인간을 살아있는 우주로 대하는 가을철의 인존人尊문화가 나오는 것입니다.

내년부터는 지구촌을 상대로 K-Spirit 문화가 나갈 것입니다. 한국의 본래 역사문화의 정수와 치유문화가 전 지구촌을 상대로 방영될 것입니다. 감사합니다.

Learn the Culture of Immortality Enlightenment

Sangjenim said, "The disaster of disease will sweep in like a powerful typhoon." This will be the point in the cosmic year of human cultivation when seeds of humanity are selected. Therefore, to ensure that not a single person in your family is lost during the disaster of disease at the time of *gaebyeok*, they must all learn the practice of Samsin meditation for receiving a Later Heaven life span.

Earth is the core of the cosmos. Every single one of us humans is a precious miracle of the universe. This is why you must be good to everyone you meet. You must treat them with respect. If you hurt someone or do them wrong, you should ask for forgiveness.

This is the point in human history when we are about to enter the cosmic autumn—the era of humanity's majesty. In the coming era, all human beings will be honored as living embodiments of the universe through the practice of Samsin meditation.

Starting next year, the K-Spirit culture will be shared with the world. In other words, the essence of Korea's original historical and healing culture will spread across the globe. Thank you.

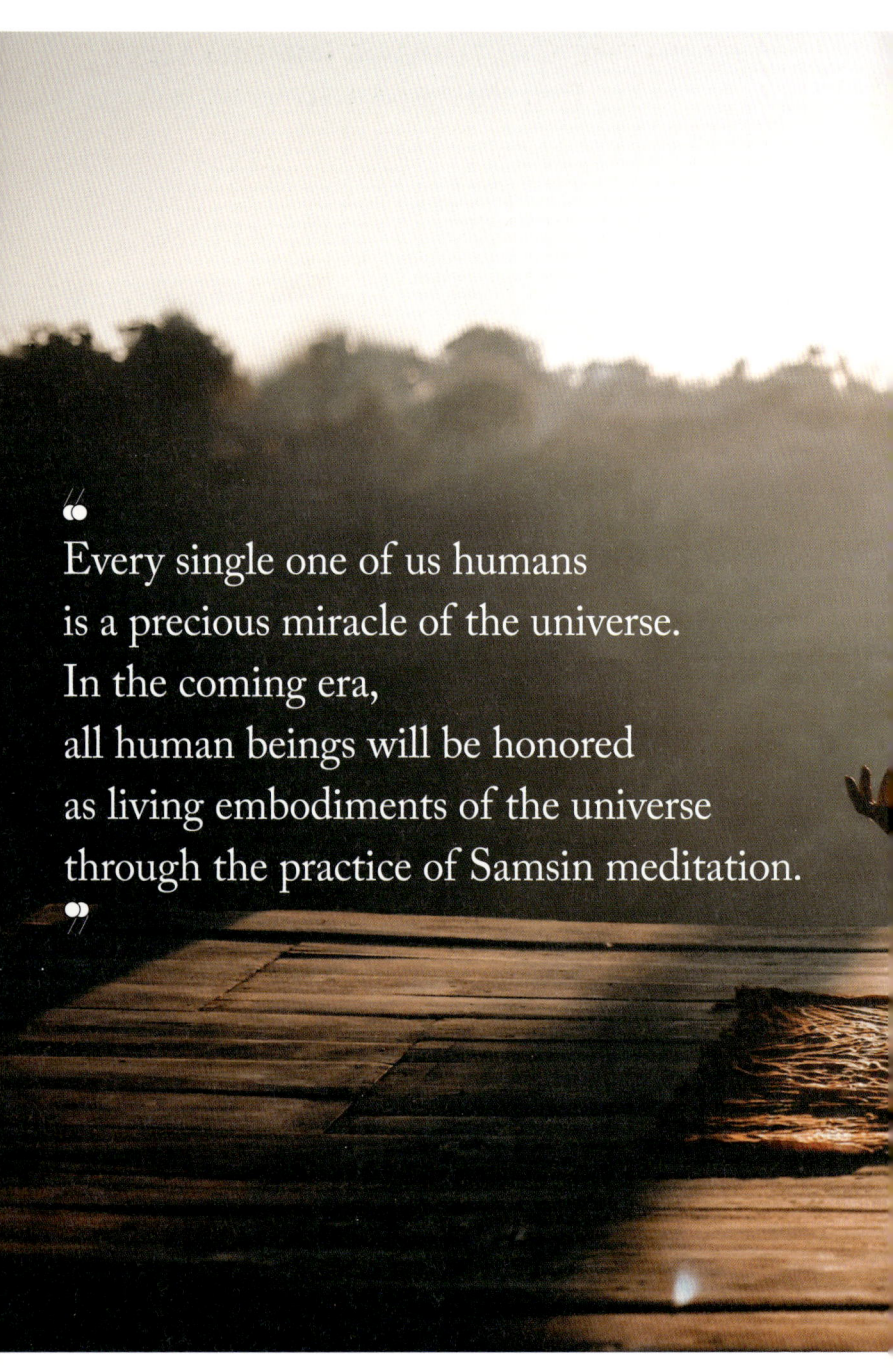

"
Every single one of us humans
is a precious miracle of the universe.
In the coming era,
all human beings will be honored
as living embodiments of the universe
through the practice of Samsin meditation.
"

저자 소개

안경전 종도사

안경전 종도사는 증산도를 이끌고 있는 최고 스승으로, 3대에 걸쳐 상제님 도업에 헌신해 온 구도자 가문에서 태어났다.

20대 초반, 깊은 명상과 사색에 몰두하여 가을개벽과 인류 문명의 대전환을 영적으로 체험하고 큰 깨달음을 얻었으며, 이를 통해 상제님 진리를 지구촌에 널리 전하려는 웅지를 품었다.

스물네 살부터 집필에 전념해 『증산도의 진리』(1980)와 『이것이 개벽이다』(1982)를 펴내며 상제님과 태모님의 무극대도를 정립했다. 이어 상제님과 태모님의 행적과 말씀을 총체적으로 집대성하는 대역사를 이끌어 1992년 『도전道典』을 간행하고, 2003년 개정판을 출간하였다.

『도전』은 영어·프랑스어·독일어·스페인어·러시아어·중국어·일본어 등으로 번역되었고, 현재 힌디어·베트남

The Supreme Master of Dao

Ahn Gyeong-jeon, the Jongdosanim ("Supreme Master of Dao"), is the head of Jeung San Do.

Unwavering faith and lifelong devotion to Sangjenim's great dao have run in the Jongdosanim's family for three generations, beginning with his grandfather and continuing with his father and himself. During his early years, the Jongdosanim's meditation and contemplation practices took him to various mountains and plains, deepening his spiritual experiences and his resolve to spread Sangjenim's truth throughout the world. In his early twenties, he spiritually experienced the great cataclysm of the Autumn Gaebyeok and its impact on the world.

At age twenty-four, the Jongdosanim began writing *Jeung San Do's Truth* to provide a comprehensive and authoritative teaching on the great dao of Sangjenim and Taemonim. This groundbreaking book was published in 1980, followed by another monumental book, *This Is Gaebyeok*, in 1982.

Since the early days of Jeung San Do, the Jongdosanim has led a massive enterprise of gathering, confirming, and compiling all records about Sangjenim and Taemonim, which culminated in the publication of the Dojeon ("Holy Scriptures of Dao") in 1992. The revised edition was published in 2003. Foreign-language editions

어·몽골어·튀르키예어·페르시아어 번역이 추진되고 있다.

1998년 상생문화연구소, 2007년 상생방송을 창립하여 우주 가을의 광명문화와 인류 원형문화의 세계화를 이끌었고, 2012년에는 9천 년 한국 역사와 문화를 담은 『환단고기』를 현대 한국어로 역주하여 세상에 내놓았다.

'빛의 문화'의 원형을 밝혀내기 위해 반세기 동안 세계 각지를 답사하여 그 결실인 '우주의 조화 빛꽃 수행'을 인류에게 전하고 있으며, 후천 가을 문명을 준비하는 상생월드센터 건립에도 힘을 기울이고 있다. 모든 이가 마음과 몸과 영혼의 어둠을 벗고 빛의 존재로 거듭나 새로운 문명의 문턱을 넘어설 수 있도록 인도하고 있다.

in English, French, German, Spanish, Russian, Japanese, and Chinese have also been published, and the Dojeon is currently being translated into Hindi, Mongolian, Vietnamese, Turkish, and Persian.

The Jongdosanim founded the Jeung San Do Sangsaeng Cultural Research Institute in 1998 and Sangsaeng Television Broadcasting in 2007.

In 2012, the Jongdosanim published a modern Korean translation and annotation of *Hwandangogi*, which is a compilation of olden texts on ancient Korean history and culture that extend back over nine thousand years.

For the past fifty years, he has journeyed across the globe to revive the lost flower of light culture from humanity's golden age. He is now sharing a vital element of the golden age culture—the Flower of Cosmic Light—with the world to help people cast darkness from their mind, body, and soul and draw in light to become beings of light before the arrival of the cosmic autumn.

국내외 주요 수행 센터 안내
Main Meditation Centers in Korea and Overseas

International Headquarters

+82-70-8644-3271 ▪ info@jeungsando.org

Korea
Seoul	+82-2-555-1691
Incheon	+82-32-429-1691
Daejeon	+82-42-254-5078
Jeonju	+82-63-211-1691
Daegu	+82-53-628-1691
Busan	+82-51-755-1691
Ulsan	+82-52-276-1691
Gangneung	+82-33-643-1349
Jeju	+82-64-721-1691

U.S.A
New York	+1-408-709-0045 ▪ jsdinus@gmail.com
Atlanta	+1-770-381-7600 ▪ jsdatlanta@gmail.com
Chicago	+1-847-921-8216 ▪ cindyoh78@gmail.com
Denver	+1-510-552-1436 ▪ hurdiane@gmail.com
Los Angeles	+1-323-937-2535 ▪ jadeflute2009@gmail.com
Virginia	+1-703-868-1870 ▪ jsdcville@gmail.com
Washington D.C.	+1-571-281-4697 ▪ washingtondc@jeungsando.org

Germany
Berlin   +49-30-3395-0577 ▪ leecy1971@gmail.com

Philippines
Manila   +63-2-7719-5075 ▪ jsdmanila@gmail.com

Indonesia
Jakarta   +62-816-131-2500 ▪ whiteheadkim@hanmail.net

JAPAN
Tokyo	+81-80-5039-8204 ▪ japan@jeungsando.org
Osaka	+81-6-6741-2047 ▪ jsd072@jsd.re.kr
Kobe	+81-78-262-1559 ▪ kobe@jeungsando.org